Edgar Cayce was born in 1877 in Hopkinsville, Kentucky and lived sixty-seven years that were sometimes painfully eventful, but tremendously enlightening. He had developed a gift in former lifetimes which gave him the capacity in this life to enter a state of altered consciousness. He was able to be in touch with the akashic records and the information in what he called the Universal Consciousness.

In his state of altered consciousness, Cayce would respond to questions and often would give special dissertations on a variety of subjects. Two thirds of his nearly 15,000 readings had to do with healing of the human body. He is well-known, too, for his predictions on earth changes and with readings on reincarnation, dreams, soul development, Christ consciousness, astrology, Atlantis, ancient Egypt, and emotional development. Cayce's readings evidenced a very close relationship with Jesus and his teachings, and it is not surprising that he advised hundreds who sought his counsel to take Jesus as their pattern for living in these troublesome times.

Cayce could also contact the unconscious mind of individuals far distant from where he was giving a reading, and could describe not only their past lives, but also the state of the inquirer's physiological functioning and what needed to be done to return that individual to full health.

Cayce's legacy for the world can be found not only in the hearts and minds of millions of individuals whose lives he has changed, but also at the Association for Research and Enlightenment (A.R.E.) Library in Virginia Beach, VA, which houses the Cayce Readings.

Edgar Cayce called his work the work of the Christ, and anyone who studies these readings in any depth will most likely agree.

William A. McGarey, M.D.

REINCARNATION

CLAIMING YOUR PAST, CREATING YOUR FUTURE

LYNN ELWELL SPARROW
WITH A FOREWORD BY CHARLES THOMAS CAYCE

St. Martin's Paperbacks

REINCARNATION: CLAIMING YOUR PAST, CREATING YOUR FUTURE

Copyright © 1988 by Lynn Elwell Sparrow

"Who Was Edgar Cayce?" copyright © 1995 by William A. McGarey, M.D.

"The Healing Work of Edgar Cayce Continues" copyright © 1995 by Mark Thurston, Ph.D.

Cover photograph by Photonica.

Library of Congress Catalog Card Number 87-46229

ISBN: 0-312-95754-8

Printed in the United States of America

Harper & Row trade paperback edition published 1988
St. Martin's Paperbacks edition/December 1995

10 9 8 7 6 5 4 3

To Scott

CONTENTS

FOREWORD

"IT IS A TIME in the earth when people everywhere seek to know more of the mysteries of the mind, the soul," said my grandfather, Edgar Cayce, from an unconscious trance from which he demonstrated a remarkable gift for clairvoyance.

His words are prophetic even today as more and more Americans in these unsettled times are turning to psychic explanations for daily events. For example, according to a national survey by the National Opinion Research Council, nearly half of American adults today believe they have been in contact with someone who has died, a figure twice that of ten years ago. Two-thirds of all adults say they have had an ESP experience; ten years ago that figure was only one-half.

Every culture throughout history has made note of its own members' gifted powers beyond the five senses. These rare individuals held special interest because they seemed able to provide solutions to life's pressing problems. America in the twentieth century is no exception.

Edgar Cayce was perhaps the most famous and most carefully documented psychic of our time. He began to use his unusual abilities when he was a young man, and from then on for over forty years he would, usually twice a day, lie on a couch, go into a sleeplike state, and respond to questions. Over fourteen thousand of these discourses, called readings, were carefully transcribed by his secretary and preserved by the Edgar Cayce Foundation in Virginia Beach, Virginia. These psychic readings continue to provide inspiration, insight, and help with healing to tens of thousands of people.

Having only an eighth-grade education, Edgar Cayce

lived a plain, simple life by the world's standards. As early as his childhood in Hopkinsville, Kentucky, however, he sensed that he had psychic ability. While alone one day he had a vision of a woman who told him he would have unusual power to help people. He also related experiences of "seeing" dead relatives. Once, while struggling with school lessons, he slept on his spelling book and awakened knowing the entire contents of the book.

As a young man he experimented with hypnosis to treat a recurring throat problem that caused him to lose his speech. He discovered that under hypnosis he could diagnose and describe treatments for the physical ailments of others, often without knowing or seeing the person with the ailment. People began to ask him other sorts of questions and he found himself able to answer these as well.

In 1910 the *New York Times* published a two-page story with pictures about Edgar Cayce's psychic ability as described by a young physician, Wesley Ketchum, to a clinical research society in Boston. From that time on people from all over the country with every conceivable question sought his help.

In addition to his unusual talents, Cayce was a deeply religious man who taught Sunday school all of his adult life and read the entire Bible once for every year that he lived. He always tried to attune himself to God's will by studying the Scriptures and maintaining a rich prayer life, as well as by trying to be of service to those who came seeking help. He used his talents only for helpful purposes. Cayce's simplicity and humility and his commitment to doing good in the world continue to attract people to the story of his life and work and to the far-reaching information he gave.

In this series we hope to provide the reader with insights in the search for understanding and meaning in life. Each book in the series explores its subject from the viewpoint of the Edgar Cayce readings and compares the perspectives of other metaphysical literature and of current scientific thought. The interested reader needs no prior knowledge of the Cayce information. When one of the Edgar Cayce readings is quoted, the identifying number of that reading is included for those who may wish to read the full text. Each volume includes suggestions for further study.

This book, *Reincarnation: Claiming Your Past, Creating Your Future* by Lynn Elwell Sparrow, explores the fascinating and challenging concepts found in the Cayce readings concerning the journey of our immortal souls through more than one life on earth. Lynn Elwell Sparrow, a former member of the staff of the Association for Research and Enlightenment and a popular lecturer on discovering your past lives, is eminently qualified to explain the ideas surrounding reincarnation, as well as karma and grace, and she does it in a very readable style that I feel sure you will enjoy.

Charles Thomas Cayce, Ph.D.
President
Association for Research and Enlightenment

ACKNOWLEDGMENTS

THE CONCEPTS EXPRESSED IN this book are largely the product of years of interaction with others who share my interest in reincarnation and its effect on our lives. I am deeply grateful to the Association for Research and Enlightenment, Inc. (A.R.E.), for providing me the rare opportunity for such interaction through travel across the United States and Canada to conduct seminars on reincarnation. I also wish to thank the hundreds of A.R.E. members who have shared their experiences and insights with me as we met together to explore our mutual interest. And I believe I speak for many when I thank the A.R.E. for maintaining the information in the Edgar Cayce readings and making it so readily available to all of us who wish to study it for ourselves.

Reincarnation as a meaningful philosophy evolved into past lives as a personal reality for me several years ago when I had the opportunity to work on a team that created a course in remembering past lives. I wish to thank Marilyn Peterson, Phyllis Embleton, and Dee Sloan—with whom I worked on that project—for the part they have played in deepening my personal experience with reincarnation.

My husband, Scott, has been a constant source of encouragement and insight to me, not only as this book found its way onto paper, but also during the far more important incubation period—years of exploring ideas together, examining and reexamining our notions of immortality. I wish to thank him for the depth of his understanding and the influence it has had on me.

Finally, I would like to thank my editor, A. Robert

Smith, for his skillful and sensitive work on the manuscript.

References to the deity using lowercase pronouns do not indicate lack of reverence by either the author or the publisher.

REINCARNATION

CLAIMING YOUR PAST,
CREATING YOUR FUTURE

Part I

A PHILOSOPHY FOR TODAY

What is life? It is a manifestation of a soul. Remember that the self is made up of body, mind, and soul. And the soul would know, does know these are all the gift of the Creator and the Maker. The purpose in life, then, is not the gratifying of the appetite nor of any selfish desire, but it is that the entity, the soul, may make the earth, where the entity finds its consciousness, a better place in which to live.

EDGAR CAYCE reading no. 4047–2

1

REINCARNATION COMES OF AGE IN THE WEST

. . . for the time has arisen in the earth when men everywhere seek to know more of the mysteries of the mind, the soul, the soul's mind . . .
EDGAR CAYCE reading no. 254–52*

REINCARNATION, ONE OF THE world's oldest and most controversial philosophies of life, is suddenly gaining widespread acceptance in the Western world. For centuries the belief that the soul survives death and returns to life in a new body has been associated primarily with Eastern religions such as Hinduism and Buddhism. And though the adherents of such reincarnationist religious systems make up two-thirds of the earth's population, the idea of rebirth has nonetheless fared poorly in mainstream Judeo-Christian tradition. A few exceptional thinkers, from Plato and Kant to Emerson and Wordsworth, have given legitimacy to the idea

---

*·Each of the Edgar Cayce readings has been assigned a two-part number to provide easy reference. Each person who received a reading was given an anonymous number; this is the first half of the two-part number. Since many individuals obtained more than one reading, the second number designates the number of that reading in the series. Reading no. 254–52 was given for a person who was assigned case number 254. This particular reading was the fifty-second one this person obtained from Cayce.

in the West; but, until recently, it has been rejected or ignored by the general population.

Today, however, serious consideration of reincarnation extends beyond the boundaries that divide East from West, philosophers from ordinary people, eccentric from acceptable. The concept of reincarnation has become a popular topic, and it has been woven into the fabric of contemporary life as an increasing number of people from a variety of backgrounds find meaning in the possibility that they have lived before. Consider the following experiences, taken from my conversations with people all across North America. They typify the ways in which a philosophy once considered foreign in our culture is rapidly entering mainstream thinking:

- A young woman tells of how, during moments of great harmony and closeness with her fiancé, she catches glimpses of another time and place. She describes the experience as one in which the present moment seems to blend with another moment in the past, and she sees herself and her loved one in seventeenth-century clothing, walking the countryside of the British Isles. These flashes of perception are so vivid that she even experiences the scents and the sounds of the imaginary setting. It doesn't happen all of the time, and the vision is only fleeting when it does occur; but she is convinced that she is not hallucinating. Instead, she understands this experience to be a flashback to a past life in which she and her fiancé were as deeply in love as they are in the present.

- A young mother, once perplexed and threatened by her four-year-old son's insistence that he used to have "another mommy and daddy," now believes that the child is remembering a past life.

She tries to normalize the flow of memory by showing the same matter-of-fact interest in her son's reports of earlier experiences that she would show if he were discussing his day at pre-school.

- A retired businessman remembers a time when belief in God seemed utterly impossible to him. How could an all-knowing, all-loving, and all-powerful deity allow a child to be born without arms, or a young man to lose his life on a battle-field thousands of miles from home? How could a just God allow some people to live in luxury, while others starve to death? And why is it that only some people find that religious faith which purports to bring eternal life? All of these questions made God a logical impossibility to this man—until he encountered the theory of rein-carnation. Now his strong belief in God is forti-fied by an understanding of our freedom to create our own circumstances over the course of many causally connected lifetimes.

- A successful paralegal with an avocation for ar-cheology cannot remember a time when ancient Egypt was not her consuming interest. At the age of four, she corrected her mother's pronuncia-tion of the name of a pharaoh. Her former gram-mar school classmates remember that her selection of subject matter for reports and class projects invariably had something to do with Egypt. Now she is beginning to wonder if this deep interest springs from a former life.

- A psychologist includes the possibility of past-life traumas in his understanding of his patients' dif-ficulties. In his personal experience, he has gained insight concerning one of his own child-hood fears—an obsessive conviction that he would die in a war—by placing it in the context of a past life. His breakthrough in insight came in early adulthood, when he had an unusually vivid dream of being a World War II pilot who was shot down over Europe. He does not suggest the possibility of reincarnation to his clients, but he nonetheless finds that his own longer-term perspective helps him select effective therapeutic interventions for them.

- A woman is caught in a destructive relationship in which she repeatedly sacrifices her own needs to her boyfriend's selfish demands. She is not sure whether she even believes in reincarnation, but the bond with this man is so strong that she decides to explore past-life connections through hypnotic regression. Under hypnosis, she goes back a hundred years to a life in France in which this man was her son. She comes out of the regression still not entirely sure about reincarnation, but with greater insight concerning the destructive dynamic of a relationship in which one does all of the giving and the other does all of the taking.

- A college student who once felt victimized by social injustices tells how his entire outlook on life was changed when he picked up his first book on reincarnation. All of his life he had been blaming other people or society as a whole for his misfortunes and lost opportunities. But when he read about reincarnation and the principle that every experience in life comes as the result of our own prior choices, he "knew" inside that this was true of his own disappointments. With that realization came the conviction that he had equal power to create a better future for himself. Since that time, the entire tenor of his life has changed for the better.

Each of these accounts represents one of the ways that people are finding reincarnation to be the most likely and most helpful explanation for the things they are experiencing in their lives. Although reincarnation is still not embraced by the majority, public opinion polls indicate that today some fifty million Americans do accept the concept. As celebrities and other respected public figures reveal their belief in reincarnation, it is becoming a topic of interest everywhere—from television talk shows to neighborhood barbecues. We are clearly living in a time when people who once kept their ideas about the soul's immortality to themselves feel more free to discuss their views openly. Even those who once rejected the notion of reincarnation seem to be reconsidering. Most significant of all, perhaps, even people who still cannot accept reincarnation personally are less likely nowadays to laugh at those of us who do. Having lectured and taught courses related to reincarnation for a number of years, I have noticed greater openness recently, for instance, on the part of the journalists who occasionally attend a past-life seminar in order to report on the event. The subject of past lives, once thought bizarre, is now treated more seriously by the media because they recognize that many of their readers or viewers are sincerely interested. What could be more indicative of the change in climate with respect to reincarnation than the sight of a well-known television journalist respectfully interviewing Shirley MacLaine on her beliefs?

Yes, reincarnation seems to have taken the Western world by storm. Yet, although belief in rebirth may appear to be the latest fad to attain overnight popularity, its climb to prominence has actually been slow and difficult. Despite its long and venerable history among the world's religious philosophies, for many years reincarnation was relegated in our culture to the domain of overly rouged psychics in flowing robes, who sat in rooms dark-

ened by heavy brocade drapes and spoke in exotic ac-
cents about strange adventures in other times and
places. When reincarnation was used as a theme in films
and novels, it was usually to amuse or horrify, not to be
taken seriously. In the interests of drama, such plots
usually centered around past lives in which death—
more specifically, murder—was the dominant theme.
Frequently, Hollywood's version of reincarnation was a
confusing mixture of past-life memory and possession—
characters who experienced flashbacks of memory
turned out to be enmeshed in the spirit and past experiences of *someone else,* who was dead.

Such portrayals were often the only exposure that
many people had to the philosophy of reincarnation. As
a result, the popular notion of rebirth was clouded with
some unfortunate distortions. Because dramas about reincarnation tended to deal with murder and untimely
death in one's past as the reasons for the stirring of
memories in the present, the impression lingered that
reincarnation is something only troubled people experience. It often became associated with only the tragedies
and dark side of life, and was seen as relating only to
those of us who have some sleeping horror in our memories. The awakening of past-life memory was depicted
as an extremely fatalistic occurrence that forced people
to go back over the same troubled ground again and
again.

In contrast, the philosophy of reincarnation that en-
gages widespread interest today is far more spiritually
and psychologically oriented. It has more to do with
such ordinary human concerns as relationships, greater
self-understanding, and learning to overcome bad habits, and less to do with the occult. It has more to do with
life than with death. Ironic though it may sound, today's
philosophy of reincarnation is more down to earth. It
asks questions about who we really are, both individu-
ally and collectively. It encourages us to take responsi-

bility for our development as spiritual beings who have a job to do in this life. It probes the deeper motivations behind human behavior and offers understandings that go beyond the mechanistic explanations of materialism on the one hand or the inflexibility of some traditional religious systems on the other. Most exciting of all, it affirms life and progress rather than death and regression.

I have called these qualities the characteristics of *today's* philosophy of reincarnation because they tend to represent the tone of what we now most often hear when reincarnation is discussed. Yet they are not the new discovery of our day. They are rather the rediscovery of the very principles that have made reincarnation such a viable philosophy of life through many centuries and in many cultures. There is little point in recapping the history of reincarnation here. It has already been compiled in several excellent publications that trace the belief in reincarnation through world cultures, both Eastern and Western, and offer a survey of illustrious figures from the fields of science, religion, literature, and statecraft who have embraced reincarnation as part of their personal worldview. Most serious students of reincarnation will want to study these works in their entirety.*

My purpose here, however, is not to examine the case for reincarnation, as though we were weighing the evidence in order to decide if it is true. As important as that line of inquiry is (and certainly anyone seriously considering reincarnation *will* have to weigh the evidence), my focus is on another equally important aspect

---

* One of the most comprehensive of these works is *Reincarnation in World Thought,* edited by Joseph Head and S. L. Cranston (New York: Julian Press, 1967). I refer readers who are interested in studying reincarnation in world thought to this excellent anthology of pertinent texts.

of reincarnation inquiry: when we *do* embrace the belief
that the soul returns after death to another physical life,
how does this belief affect our lives? Just what does the
philosophy of reincarnation accomplish in our experience after it has taken root? And, more basically still,
just exactly what *does* the philosophy of reincarnation
teach? The core idea that the soul returns to earth may
be simple enough, but from that point on the theory
gets a lot more complicated. Here is where we can turn
to the work of Edgar Cayce for some enlightening insights.

EDGAR CAYCE'S CONTRIBUTION TO OUR UNDERSTANDING OF REINCARNATION

Edgar Cayce has often been suggested as the primary
catalyst behind the growing acceptance of reincarnation
in Western culture today. Like most of the current
trends that Cayce anticipated in the unorthodox content
of his readings, reincarnation was hardly an American
institution when he first spoke of it more than sixty
years ago. It was 1923 when Cayce, who had been giving
psychic medical readings for some twenty years, surprised himself and most of the people close to him by
bringing up the subject of reincarnation at the close of
one of his readings.

Admittedly, Cayce knew before he began the reading
that he was about to plumb the depths of his source for
a new kind of information. A prosperous businessman
named Arthur Lammers had brought him to Dayton,
Ohio for the express purpose of giving a new kind of
reading. Lammers, who had taken an interest in Cayce's
astounding record of accuracy with physical readings (at
that point, the only kind of reading he gave), had reasoned that a source which demonstrated such accuracy
concerning things that could be verified would be the

ideal place to turn for answers to some of life's more abstract questions. Because Lammers's own search had recently led him to the study of astrology, it was an astrological birth chart, or horoscope, that he asked for now. He hoped that the sleeping Cayce would be able to attain a level of precision with respect to astrological conditions at the time of birth that he had been unable to obtain using normal birth records and mathematical calculations. Sure enough, even though the conscious Cayce knew nothing about astrology, the sleeping Cayce gave a point-by-point dissertation, describing how astrological aspects at birth related to inclinations of character. As a further development of this aspect of the reading, Cayce volunteered the information, "He was once a monk," at the end of the astrological assessment.

If the idea of reincarnation seems foreign and raises controversy in our time, imagine how the idea would have struck America in the 1920s! It had taken Cayce a good part of the twenty years during which he had been giving health readings to come to terms with the strange ability that turned him into a veritable medical encyclopedia when he was "asleep." He had wrestled with the nature of his ability; he had wrestled with the content of what he said, always concerned about the possibility of causing harm through the advice his readings gave. A man of traditional Protestant upbringing and values, Cayce was just barely holding on to the last vestiges of "normality" in the face of his strange ability to give clairvoyant medical readings. Now here he was suggesting that reincarnation, of all things, was the means by which life advanced.

Only Arthur Lammers, whose personal search had led him to explore virtually all of the major religions and philosophies of the world, saw beyond the temporary turmoil the reading's revelation had unleashed. For Lammers, it was the beginning of a grand inquiry into life's most important questions. For Cayce, it was another in a series of challenges to come to grips with the strange ability he had never asked for. While we all must carefully evaluate the philosophy and weigh the evidence before we can take a reasoned position with regard to reincarnation, for Cayce, this process was intensified to crisis proportions because of the personal responsibility he felt for bringing these concepts through in his own psychic readings. An awful power and an awful responsibility was involved in ushering in what would be a revolutionary view of reality for most people in his circle of acquaintance and beyond. Cayce was savvy enough to recognize that readings about reincarnation would not only fan the flames of controversy about his work in some quarters, but would also promote acceptance of the belief in other quarters. It was probably this latter potential that he found most sobering, for a conscientious desire not to mislead was his highest priority.

Nevertheless, the possibilities raised by that first reference to reincarnation were not of the sort that Cayce could just turn his back on them and continue his life as though they had never come up. He had to find out if they were true. And so, using a principle that the readings were later to recommend to many a seeker, Cayce kept his mind as open as possible while testing the validity of these new concepts in his own life. First he gathered more information. Additional readings were taken to ask for clarification of what the original reading had suggested about rebirth. The information in those readings—which were given for Cayce, his family, and his close associates—was compared with what could be known about those same people from other sources. Repeatedly, the readings offered insightful angles on situations and personal traits that were indeed aspects of the lives of the people under consideration. Regarding the philosophy itself as it unfolded in these readings, Cayce turned to his trusted Bible to evaluate reincarnation's compatibility with what he read there. Finally, he began to explore what some of the great thinkers in history had to say on the subject.

Cayce's inquiry did in time lead to his own conviction that reincarnation was a valid philosophy of life, and a whole new category of psychic readings was born. Over the next twenty-one years, Cayce gave a total of 2,500 readings about reincarnation to some 1,500 people. Called "life readings," these psychic discourses offered comprehensive portraits of the inner person, describing relevant experiences from past lives and outlining pertinent mental, emotional, and spiritual patterns that arose from these experiences. The life readings even traced physical conditions to origins in past lives.

The readings wove a fascinating tapestry of connectedness among people who returned to earth again and again in an ever-changing configuration of relationships with one another. They laid out the larger drama of human existence from the perspective of individual souls who had lived in ancient Atlantis before it was destroyed, had helped build the Great Pyramid in Egypt, or had seen the coming of Jesus one starlit Bethlehem night. The souls whose history was laid out in the life readings had participated in the founding of such cultural forces as the Jewish nation, the Roman Empire, the Christian church, and the United States government, to name just a few. Virtually every historical epoch is described somewhere in these readings, and always from the vantage point of the specific human lives that were involved and affected.

Today, Cayce's readings continue to offer a unique contribution to our understanding of the process of reincarnation and the implications it holds concerning everyday life. At the very least, they provide one of the largest collections of reincarnation case histories available anywhere. As we shall see throughout this book, these case histories offer us far more than the records of other people's experience. From the experience of others and from the light that is shed on that experience in the commentary of their life readings, we can derive principles that apply to our own experience as well. Thus the Cayce readings offer us the raw material for turning abstract theory into a living, personal philosophy of life.

In the pages of the Cayce life readings we can find a detailed understanding of just what reincarnation is all about. We see why it happens and how it happens. We are shown the workings of the law of karma (or cause and effect), and we learn how it determines the kind of experiences we have in life. We are invited to undertake a fascinating search for knowledge of our own past lives, and we are shown how to go about that search. As we explore these concepts, Cayce's strongly practical approach to reincarnation serves as a constant reminder to ask ourselves, "What does this mean to me?" This question will always be at the heart of our approach to these subjects.

This material also gives us much to chew on with respect to some of the biggest questions in life: What is the soul? Where does it come from? Why are we here in the first place and where are we headed? Enough information is put forth on these great riddles of existence to occupy an inquisitive mind for a lifetime, at least! The life readings expand our frame of reference beyond the earth alone, suggesting that the entire solar system and ultimately the universe make up our true spiritual home. Universal laws, every bit as reliable as their physical-law counterparts, are described and their influence on the experience of souls explained. Nothing less mysterious than the origin and destiny of life itself is the real subject matter of these readings. This, too, we will attempt to distill into some basic understandings, while at the same time recognizing that the truths we will probe can never be contained in the pages of this or any other book.

Finally, beyond any contribution the life readings make to our understanding and to our capacity to live life constructively, they inspire us with a vision of our true purpose and the ultimate goodness of existence. They describe a universe animated not only by universal laws and forces, but by the inexhaustible love of its Creator. They present an existence in which every one of us is loved and cared for by the One who is the ultimate power and reality behind all that is. The message in these readings is one of hope that is extended to every human being, no matter what his or her current circumstances. In the final analysis, the life readings present a joyous story that calls us to claim a spiritual heritage far richer than most of us would dare imagine for ourselves. It is this perspective that stands out in my mind as Edgar Cayce's most important contribution to the literature of reincarnation.

2
WHAT *IS* REINCARNATION?

What then, the entity asks, is a soul? What does it look like? What is its plane of experience or activity? How may ye find one? It may not be separated in a material world from its own place of abode in the body-physical, yet the soul looks through the eyes of the body—it handles with the emotion of the sense of touch—it may be aware through the factors in every sense and thus adds to its body just as food of the material world has made for a growing physical body in which the soul may and does indeed dwell in its passage or activity during any individual phase of an experience in the earth.

EDGAR CAYCE reading no. 487–17

WHAT IS REINCARNATION? In addressing this question there is a temptation to begin at the beginning and tell the story of the soul in the earth—that is, to tell how we came to be involved in physical existence in the first place, and what we've been doing during the thousands of years that humankind has been on this planet. Yet, fundamental as that story may be to our grasp of who we are and why we are here, we must first define the term reincarnation before the story of the soul in the earth can truly become our own story.

What It Means to Incarnate

In simplest terms, the theory of reincarnation suggests that the soul returns to human existence again and again, through the normal cycle of birth and death, for the purpose of its own development. In order truly to understand reincarnation, however, we must start with a sense of what it means to incarnate. This step may seem straightforward enough but in fact it is fraught with confusion.

The problem is that simple definitions of the terms "reincarnate" and "incarnate" do not adequately convey the wonder and mystery of spirit expressing itself through matter. We can learn from the dictionary that to incarnate means to clothe with flesh and bodily form, but this gives us little sense of what it is that *gets* clothed in flesh or how that which is clothed in the flesh relates to the very flesh which clothes it. Yet these are the real questions we must answer if we are to understand reincarnation, for they hold the key to our comprehension of who and what we are and why we are here. Let's look first, then, at what it is that does the incarnating. Then we can go on to explore the process of incarnation—and reincarnation—itself.

What Is It That Incarnates?

When we ask this question, we are really asking *who we are.* If some part of us survives bodily death and is able to return to physical existence in a different body, who or what is that part?

The obvious answer to this question is the soul. Any explanation of reincarnation will tell us that it is the soul that takes on a succession of bodies in its journey through the earth. It is a cornerstone of the philosophy of reincarnation that we are souls who occupy bodies rather than bodies who have souls. But since so much of our conscious identity rests with our physical and conscious, reflecting selves, this notion of ourselves as souls can seem abstract at best and so remote at times as to become meaningless. If the awareness of ourselves as souls is to have any meaning for us on a day-to-day basis, we must have a clearer sense of what the soul is—what it is made up of and how it relates to the physical body and conscious selves we are already so at home with. Here the Edgar Cayce readings offer some helpful clarification, and so here we shall begin.

The first premise we find in the Cayce readings regarding our essential nature has to do not with us alone, but with the fact that *we are connected to the God who has made us.* The essence of who we are springs from the eternal, limitless essence of all existence. In the philosophic system developed in these readings, that essence is both universal and personal. In its universal connotation, it is most often called "Creative Force" or "Creative Forces." In its personal connotation, it is called God and it is called the Father. And, due to conventions of expression rather than to any conviction that the deity is male, the readings use the personal pronouns "He," "Him," and "His" when referring to God in the personal connotation. Consequently, I will alternately use universal and personal terminology, including the male personal pronoun, to describe the ultimate power behind all of life, depending upon which connotation seems best to fit the concept.*

---

* Readers who object to any of the terms I use in reference to God may substitute words with which they are more comfortable. I do not know of a word that is broad enough to encompass all that God is, nor altogether free of problematic associations. Therefore, we will attempt to forge an overall understanding by using a variety of terms used by Edgar Cayce and others to describe the Creator of this universe.

Using the personal terminology, then, we are told that a part of our Creator is at the core of each one of us. This is the part of us, according to Cayce, that is made in the image of God. This is also the part of us that we would call *spirit*. Switching to language with more of the universal connotation, spirit is the essence of all life; the part of our individual makeup that is the basic life force of our very being we would call spirit as well. A very simple way to express this concept would be to say that spirit is the stuff of which we are made, the essence of our being.

The second premise is that *we are individuals*. Not only are we part of the larger reality from which we derive our being, but we also have an individuality of consciousness. We have the capacity to shape or pattern our spiritual essence into unique expression. This capacity to create, shape, or pattern the expression or manifestation of spirit in individual form is called *mind*. "Spirit taketh form in the mind," we are told in one reading (no. 3359–1). "Mind becomes the builder," this same reading goes on to say; and here we encounter one of the most important principles we can ever know concerning our deepest nature: with the mind we literally create our reality.

The creative power of the mind is emphasized in so many ways throughout the Cayce readings that it may well be the single most important thing we can know about ourselves. "Mind is the builder," we are told again and again. Our thoughts not only create the internal realities that cause us to respond in certain ways to the world around us; they are also a real force that goes out from us to affect external realities.

"Thoughts are things," these readings insist, and they may create "crimes or miracles" (no. 5680–1). There is no such thing as an idle thought, for so-called idle thoughts are the building blocks of more complex patterns of thinking. For example, individual thoughts of love and compassion add to the loving and compassionate patterns that have been built in our minds by previous loving and compassionate thoughts, while thoughts of greed or malice or lust just as surely latch on to *their* thought-pattern counterparts in our minds. Thought patterns grow with feeding; and as thought patterns grow, they gather a momentum that will eventually find expression in material reality. But here we get ahead of ourselves, for we are not yet ready to explore our interaction with material reality. We must first finish developing a working understanding of our essential nature.

So far, then, we have seen that the root of our nature is spirit and that with the mind we shape our spiritual essence into individual expression. This brings us to the third aspect of our essential nature as it is presented in the Cayce material. Not only are we individuated spirits, but *we are endowed with free will.* At the core of our very nature, we possess the right *and* the responsibility to choose. We choose what the mind will create out of the raw material of spirit, and we choose which of the mind's creations we will activate at any moment in our experience.

A good analogy to help illustrate the difference between the mind's creating, patterning capacity and the will's choosing capacity may be found in the relationship between an actor and a director. The actor's careful study of a role involves learning not only a particular character's lines, but getting to the heart of that character's feelings and motivations. An actor who has truly learned a role will have acquired an entire complex of reactions and habits and forms of expression that are consistent with what the character is all about. The actor's patterning of himself or herself to create an entire role is like the mind's creative patterning capacity—except, of course, that in the case of our mind's creations, we are not only the actor who rehearses; we are also the playwright who creates the role in the first place. The director, on the other hand, determines the appropriateness of the actor's expression and guides it to fit the needs of the production. This is like the function of the will, which has supervisory control over the expression of the mind's creations. Sometimes the will chooses wisely, sometimes unwisely; but it is always the part of ourselves that directs the play.

To carry our analogy a step further, an actor will learn an assortment of roles over the course of a lifetime, and all will be there within his or her bank of experience. These various roles are like the mental creations that are there in pattern within us. In using the analogy of a role, however, I do not mean to imply insincerity. The roles we have created for ourselves consist of actual patterns of thinking and response to life that we have built with our minds. For example, the "Someone has hurt my feelings, so I am going to feel sorry for myself" role is a very popular one, which we genuinely live at times. The "With my luck, it will probably turn out all wrong" role appeals to us when we are in a self-defeating frame of mind. There are positive roles as well. The "I know I can do it if I really try" role is one example of the kind of mind pattern that works wonders when we want to get a job done.

We can understand virtually every aspect of the way we respond to life's various opportunities and challenges in terms of these mind-patterns. We have rehearsed these roles over the course of our experience, life after life, to the point where they have become real aspects of ourselves, and so here the analogy to a mere role breaks down. These patterns of mind relate to winning or losing responses to life situations; but they also touch the inner realities behind those superficial orientations. They touch our deepest values and motivations. As the mind continually builds these patterns, our thoughts either gravitate toward concern with ourselves and our own needs, or toward caring for others. The response patterns we build with our minds have to do with whether our priorities are on temporal and material gratifications, or whether they are on eternal and spiritual ones. In the final analysis, they have to do with whether our patterns of mind are directed toward or away from our essential connectedness with God. As such, they are not only the means through which we succeed or fail in this life; but they are the means through which our souls are either enriched or impoverished. This is where the will comes in to the picture.

Following our actor-director analogy, it is with the will that we choose which roles we will enact, how we will enact them, and under what circumstances. Just as the director guides an actor's expression and directs the actor's interpretation of his or her role, it is with the will that we direct the tremendous creative capacity of the mind. The will directs it to create patterns that are either constructive or destructive. It is with the will that we choose to draw on the best within ourselves, or merely the mediocre, or even the worst. In short, the will is the aspect of our essential nature that reflects the freedom that our Creator has given us to shape our own destinies.

It is important to remember that the foregoing is a description of who we are at the nonphysical core of our being. Spirit, mind, and will together make up what is generally called the *soul.* This is the part of us that is eternal, and which experiences the succession of lives we call reincarnation. The term Edgar Cayce most often used in his readings to describe this core identity that survives bodily death was *soul-entity,* or sometimes just *entity.* It is also referred to in some places in the readings as the *spiritual body,* which emphasizes the coherent, whole quality that the soul possesses, independent of a physical body to give it form. Still, that physical existence is far from unimportant, for it provides the window through which we can become more fully aware of our souls. It is to this physical existence, this process of incarnating, that we now turn our attention.

The Soul Incarnate

Ideally, the process of becoming incarnate, of taking on physical form, would be a straightforward matter of a spiritual body (the soul) expressing itself in a material world through the medium of the human form. Indeed, this is essentially what is implied when we liken the process of taking on a flesh body to getting into a car and driving it, or putting on clothes. The car and the clothing are not the self, but merely the vehicle or garb of the self.

Yet the soul's bonds to physical existence are usually far more entangled than the automobile or wardrobe analogies might lead us to believe. Becoming incarnate involves more than merely occupying a physical form. Becoming incarnate means temporarily becoming *one* with a physical form. And as long as we are one with a physical form and the material existence that goes with it, the only direct knowledge we have of ourselves comes through our consciousness while in a flesh body.

That consciousness is several steps removed from the consciousness of the soul-entity described above, for it reflects an accumulation of patterns and choices we have built over time, and which we may figuratively describe as forming layers of distortion between our conscious awareness and our deeper identity. We sometimes call these layers by such names as "personality" and "ego"; but regardless of the name we give them, they represent our self-created sense of self rather than our true identity at the soul level. This is why, coherent and complete as our soul identity may be in the nonmaterial realm, it may still seem a bit distant to us from our vantage point here in materiality.

Another way to describe the soul's tendency to become submerged in the identity of physical existence is to say that we have come to identify ourselves with our creations rather than with our own core nature. Like the woman who knows herself only in terms of the position she holds in a large corporation, or the man whose sense of identity depends upon his ability to maintain status in his community, we have come to confuse the creations of personality, ego, and physical existence with our deeper knowledge of who we are. When every day we see people losing their true identities in the false identities of their roles, possessions, and passing pleasures, we are seeing the human condition in bold relief: for this is a picture of how we as souls have lost much of our awareness of who we truly are through false identification with our creations.

It does not have to be this way. Just as our experience in the earth can be one of submerging our spiritual identity in materiality, it can also be one of infusing materiality with spiritual identity. This is one of the great challenges of life in the earth, and it also points up the centerpiece of reincarnation theory: the reason that we live so many lives.

WHY DO WE REINCARNATE?

We have seen that we are spiritual beings made up of spirit, mind, and will. We know that we have the capacity to create and the freedom to choose, and we know that we can either submerge our spiritual identity in material existence or bring spiritual identity into materiality. But why? Why are we here and why do we reincarnate?

The answer to this question lies in our first premise concerning our deepest nature: connectedness with God. As explained in the Cayce material, our very reason for being is to be "companions" and "cocreators" with God. Because God wants his companions to be nothing less than peers who have chosen him just as freely as he has chosen them, we have been given free will. God does not want clones of himself or mindless lackies for his cocreators, but fully individual beings who can participate completely in the wonders of the existence he has prepared for us. The process of reincarnation provides the opportunity for us to become just such companions and cocreators, as we shall now see.

The Childhood of Our Immortality

In order to allow the development of our individuality, God created us in immature form, leaving us room to "grow up" spiritually into unique, adult companions. This, then, is the primary reason that we reincarnate. All of our experiences, life after life, are an opportunity to grow into our fullness as spiritual beings. As Goethe once put it, "Life is the childhood of our immortality."

As with any maturation process, our successive lives add the kind of depth to our understanding that only comes with experience. They give us the opportunity to learn from our mistakes. Finally, they give us the opportunities we need to develop our talents, abilities, creativity, and capacity to love.

All of this takes time. When we remember that it is God we are growing up to join, can we wonder that it takes more than the span of one life? We cannot rush this process, for to rush it would be to foreclose some important stages of growth. And each stage of growth is essential, for it is only when we complete this growth process that we will be able to claim the special role he has prepared for us. To help us understand the absolute necessity that we "grow up" spiritually before we can be true companions to God, we can look to the relationship between an earthly parent and child. There is a great difference between the level of companionship a beloved infant provides its parent, and the companionship a grown-up child is capable of providing. The wise and truly loving parent will, like God, exult in the individuality that a child eventually grows into, because it makes the child a true "other" rather than a mere reflection of self.

But growing up is a tricky thing, and many a child's quest for individuality becomes a detour into rebellion. This has certainly been true for us as souls, as we shall see in the next chapter, when we follow our collective soul history from creation to the present. Yet even our rebellion need not close the door to growth; learning can result from all of our choices in the earth.

The Arena of Choice

In simplest terms, physical life in the earth gives us the opportunity to make choices and witness the results of those choices. It is here in this life—and in every life that we have lived or will ever live in the earth—that we can learn to exercise our free will in such a way as to bring individuality rather than rebellion. The process of reincarnation has often been likened to a school for souls, in which each life represents a class that we either pass or fail. The lessons we are here to learn have to do with the way we treat other people; how we handle such issues as love, creativity, power, and sexuality; our capacity for honesty, integrity, and altruism; and ultimately our concept of ourselves as totally loved children of God who are heirs to all of creation. Those classes we fail must be repeated; those we pass lead to our eventual graduation.

The analogy of a practicum—in which we actually have the chance to practice skills and knowledge in real-life settings—is an apt description of the soul's experience in this arena of choice we call the earth plane. Life in the earth is definitely an exercise in learning by doing. We learn through direct experience that our constructive thoughts, words, and deeds lead to greater harmony in our own lives and the lives of those around us; and that our destructive thoughts, words, and deeds will just as surely bring disharmony—sooner or later.

This relationship between choices and results is the main dynamic upon which reincarnation operates. It is called the law of cause and effect; or, to use the Eastern term that comes from the Sanskrit word meaning "deed" or "act," *karma*. We will be making a detailed study of the law of karma, beginning in chapter five and continuing throughout the rest of the book. For now, let's look at the concepts that are essential to a basic understanding of this law that governs the process of reincarnation.

The Guidance System of the Law

Karma is often misconstrued as a system of punishments and rewards, with emphasis most often placed on karma as punishment for our wrongdoings: "You must have bad karma." It is understandable that such a notion would spring up, for it is true that karma brings us unpleasant and often painful experiences as a result of the destructive choices we have made in the past. Karma will just as surely bring us the benefits and the blessings of the good and constructive choices we make, which we may interpret as rewards. But even though we may experience these two versions of karma in terms of punishment and reward, it is actually a neutral force analogous to any number of physical laws. For example: we do not say that gravity is punishing us when we fall from a second-story window; nor do we say that the laws of aerodynamics are rewarding us when the plane we fly in stays airborne. We understand that these laws of gravity and aerodynamics are part of the natural order of the world we live in, and we know that it is we who determine—by our interaction with those laws—whether they will aid or harm us.

Karma is that kind of law; but instead of operating strictly in the physical world, it operates in the world of ideas, ethics, motivation, and morality. The law of cause and effect is the natural expression of the ultimate goodness and harmony of this universe, which we call God. As a force toward goodness and harmony, the action of this law will always be in the direction of maintaining that goodness and harmony. Hence constructive choices on our part seem to bring reward; they run with the flow of harmony and so they cannot help but bring more harmony. On the other hand, our destructive choices, in running counter to that natural flow of harmony, can't help but bring experiences of discord. We may call that discord punishment, but it is really nothing more than the guidance system of cause and effect putting us back on track.

A corollary is the realization that nothing happens to us that is not the product of our own choices. This is another perspective on the principle we considered earlier, which tells us that we create our own reality. Through the patterns of thinking and action that we build, we set real forces in motion in our lives. These forces will, under the undeniable law of cause and effect, bring us conditions that are consistent with what we ourselves have built.

Sometimes the choices we make bring quick results that can be easily traced to the original action. For example, a student cheats on an exam, is discovered, and receives a failing grade. Sometimes the results come quickly, but the connection to the original act is symbolic or thematic rather than literal and direct. For example, someone gives money at great sacrifice to help another person in need and then wins the lottery the next week. Other choices will build momentum for some time before the results are experienced. For example, a student cheats on an exam, gets an A, and then later in life someone takes unfair advantage of him by cheating. Or, a person gives at great sacrifice to help others whose need is even greater, and never rises financially above the bare subsistence level. Yet, in a future life, that individual is born into wealth and ease.

Because we do not know what has gone before in our own experience and the experience of those around us, "fate" can look capricious—dealing hands of toil, inner turmoil, or suffering to some, while dealing good fortune to others. But the law of cause and effect tells us that nothing happens that is not of our own choosing. More important still, it tells us that nothing happens which is not ultimately conducive to our own good and growth.

These two points are central to our understanding of karma: we have chosen all that happens to us, and we can grow through every experience life brings our way. But if they are central points, they are also points that can give rise to overly simplistic and even glib responses to life's difficulties and life's tragedies. For this reason, I encourage those readers who are new to the philosophy of reincarnation to take the preceding discussion of karma as merely an overview of a central element in thinking about reincarnation, rather than as a pat rationalization of life's sorrows. We will probe the more complex questions that arise concerning karma and human suffering in subsequent chapters. For now, though, let's complete this encapsulated version of the philosophy of reincarnation by reviewing what we can say about the ultimate purpose behind it all.

The Destiny of the Soul

We have already seen that a state of spiritual maturity, in which we will be fit companions for the God of this universe, is the end toward which our experience is unfolding. It is difficult—if not impossible—to get a clear sense of what this state will be like, for it will be unlike any state of being known to our conscious, physical selves. The Cayce readings tell us that we know ourselves to be ourselves, and yet we will be one with the greater reality we call God or Creative Forces. No annihilation of selfhood is implied here; rather, we will come to know our true Self as we have never known it before. We will discard the false selves of personality and ego that we have created, and will come to identify with and replace them with a knowledge of ourselves as eternal, spiritual beings who share in the love, wisdom, creativity, peace, and joy that come with being one with the God of this universe. We will, in a sense, go "home"— back to our source. But when we go back, it will be as souls who are older, wiser, and more complete than we were when it all began. And so, perhaps, our best vision of where we are headed comes now in looking at where we have come from.

3
How Did It All Get Started?

In the beginning all souls were as a unity to the God-Force. As self added or subtracted that which was in keeping with God's purpose, ye added or subtracted from the blessings ye might be conscious of in materiality. Thus karma is builded. And the law is perfect—what ye sow ye reap. There is no law causing man to separate himself from his Maker. There is no cause except man's own indulgence or neglect.

EDGAR CAYCE reading no. 3660–1

THE STORY OF THE soul's entrance into the earth, as told in the Edgar Cayce life readings, is an epic rivaling anything that Hollywood has yet dreamed up. What's more, it is our story—the sleeping history nestled somewhere within the consciousness of every human being. As such, it has the potential to awaken inner realizations that mere theory can never evoke. Read it as a great myth, or read it as a literal past. In either case, the universal, eternal values it deals with are the same.

"BEFORE THE BEGINNING"

Whenever we try to talk about the beginning of life, we run up against an impenetrable wall of mystery. No matter how far back we go in our conceptualizing, we always reach that point at which we have no answer to the question of where life and the universe came from. When we say that God created it all, we are stuck with the unanswerable question of where God came from. When we opt for such scientific explanations as the "big bang" theory, we are left just as much in the dark concerning the origin of those conditions that eventually led to the big bang.

The unanswerable questions surrounding the origins of reality and the beginning of time stand as monuments to our helplessness in the face of life's ultimate questions. In a sense, they are a constant reminder that reality is far larger than anything of which we can conceive; therefore we should not limit our notion of reality only to those things we can understand. Nor should we fool ourselves into thinking we can solve life's mysteries simply by reducing them to simplistic explanations.

Nonetheless, we experience the drive to understand the reality we live in as fully as possible, and we often feel compelled to make coherent sense out of those things that are most mysterious. I do not pretend that the story of life given in the Cayce readings breaks through these age-old barriers to our comprehension, but it does offer us at least the rudiments of a coherent understanding. Like the theologian who begins with God or the scientist who begins with the big bang, we must choose a place to begin. We must reach back as far as possible before hitting that impenetrable wall of mystery, and begin from there. It is all we can do.

The Cayce readings tell us that we were created as souls long before we ever came into physical existence. We were with God as he brought his created universe into manifestation. As it is rather poetically expressed in one reading, we were with him "when the morning stars sang together." Not only were we with God, but we were actually *extensions* of God, portions of his very essence: "Hence as He moved, souls—portions of Himself—came into being."

We were created to be companions and we were given formative power over ourselves in order that we might be fully individualized. The entire universe was our field of activity, and we went out into it as children might venture out into the world in order to find themselves. And so we began our exploration of the universe, endowed with the creative capacity of the mind and the choosing freedom of the will.

In our prephysical state, we could literally create with our minds the way a child can build things with sand on the beach. In our movement in consciousness through the realms of God's creation, we were free to interact fully with whatever we encountered. Some of what we encountered was part of the physical world that was coming into form. Some of what we encountered belonged to other, nonmaterial planes of reality that even today defy our conscious comprehension. But just as we live in a three-dimensional world in which reality is defined according to the physical dimensions of height, width, and depth, there are four-, five-, and six-dimensional worlds (and untold numbers of other dimensions) in which reality is defined according to entirely different constructs.

Throughout these planes of reality we moved in consciousness, discovering the many dimensions of the universe the way an infant discovers its fingers and its toes and its nose. And with that discovery came the realization that we could also manipulate the realities we encountered, using our creative capacity to create in the medium of whatever dimension we found ourselves in. Among those realities we experienced was the three-dimensional earth plane. Here, the medium we could manipulate with our creativity was materiality.

COMING INTO THE EARTH

From the start, the earth seemed to hold a special fascination for us. Perhaps it was the thrill of seeing the creations of our minds take three-dimensional form. Perhaps it was the beauty of the natural world. Perhaps it was the intensity of experience that material existence brings. Whatever it was, the allure was irresistible to souls. Our capacity to participate in materiality became an all-encompassing obsession. Deeper and deeper our awareness of who we really were became submerged as a materially oriented consciousness took over. As free, creative, nonphysical beings, we had the power to link our consciousness with the life taking place on this planet, thus vicariously experiencing fleshly existence. With the creative power of mind, souls were actually able to project creations of thought into materiality. These creations the Cayce readings call *thought forms*. The more we merged our consciousness with the physical life that was taking place on the earth plane, and the more we created physical extensions of ourselves in materiality, the less we were able to remember our true nature as souls.

It is not that it was wrong for souls to include the earth plane among their experiences. As part of God's creation, and as part of the universe that we were free to roam, the earth held valuable opportunities for souls to explore the depths of creativity and the expression of spirit in matter. It was also not wrong for souls to interact with materiality. The problem was that souls became so completely engrossed in materiality that they lost consciousness of their connection with God. They lost their awareness of themselves as children of God and replaced it with an awareness of self as a material being. Eventually, souls became entrapped in their self-made prisons of material existence. Expressing in materiality through their thought forms, souls became lost, like children thoroughly confused by an amusement park hall of mirrors. So complete was their immersion in materiality that they didn't even know they were lost. The great detour of rebellion had begun.

THE COMING OF ADAM

All of this took place before human beings ever walked the face of the earth. Except for those physical forms that souls took on and created for themselves, there was still no fleshly component to our makeup. It is also important to clarify that, even though I have referred to the events surrounding souls' initial descent into material consciousness as being "our" experience, these events in truth involved *some* rather than *all* souls. As that first influx of souls became increasingly lost in the experience of materiality, other souls still maintained an awareness of who they were in relation to God. This group of souls became part of God's plan of rescue for the souls who had lost their way in the earth.

Just as free will was the only acceptable means through which souls could grow into their full individuality, it had to be by free choice and not coercion that the materially bound souls reawakened to their true nature as children of God. The plan was for those souls who had not yet lost their God-consciousness to come into the earth in order to remind their wayward fellow souls of who they really were. This second influx of souls needed a vehicle of physical expression in order to reach those souls who were by now so encased in physical form that it had become their only sense of identity. And so the human body was perfected by God as the optimum physical channel through which a soul could manifest in the earth.

From the readings' discussion of this phase of our

experience, we can infer that various life forms were evolving on the earth at that time, among them the precursors of human beings. God "adapted" this prehuman form to be the perfect vehicle for souls entering material existence. The readings are emphatic that this process involved an upward evolution of form rather than a downward "descent" from a known species such as the monkey. Thus Adam and Eve came into the earth as the first souls to inhabit human bodies.

We're told in the readings that Adam and Eve were representative of all of humankind, which actually appeared on the earth in five places at once, as the red, white, black, brown, and yellow races of the human family. Although the geography of the earth has altered significantly since that time, the actual spots on the globe were roughly correlated with those areas we would now call the Gobi Desert, India, Europe, South America, and western North America.

The coming of souls in human form also meant the beginning of our experience as males and females. On the deepest level of our soul identity, we are androgynous beings, possessing both "male" and "female" qualities (as we would label them from our earthly perspective). Yet the experience of life in the earth, with its polarities of male and female, required a similar polarizing of qualities within the soul. The readings do not specify exactly what this process involved, but it seemed to entail the simultaneous emphasis of one pole and deemphasis of the other within the same soul. Thus to enter a male body, the male aspects were emphasized and the female deemphasized. Similarly, the androgynous soul, in entering the physical form of the female, would suppress its male aspects and express its female aspects. Over the course of many incarnations, this process was to be reversed many times, with souls sometimes entering male bodies and experiencing their male-dominant qualities, and in other lives experiencing their female-dominant qualities while in female bodies. Through this bipolar experience, both sets of qualities could be brought to their fullest and best expression. But here we get ahead of ourselves, for we are still considering what happened when that second influx of souls first appeared in the earth as the human race.

Their purpose for coming in, as we have seen, was to lead the wayward souls home. And though they were collectively called Adam and Eve, there were also two spiritual entities—an individual Adam and an individual Eve—who led this rescue mission. The course of this mission did not run smoothly, however, and soon this second group of souls began to lose themselves in materiality as well. According to Cayce, this is the Genesis story generally called "the fall of man." The departure of Adam and Eve from paradise is the allegorical story of this group of souls who lost their way and forgot why they had come into the earth in the first place.

Some of the souls from the second influx eventually intermingled with the original group and with the physical forms those souls had created for themselves, giving physical birth to strange mixtures of human and beast. Images of these half-human, half-beast creatures survive today in such mythological beings as centaurs and the Minotaur. To draw another parallel to the story of humankind found in Genesis, this was when "the sons of God saw the daughters of men that they were fair; and they took them wives . . ." (Genesis 6:2). As we're told later in this same chapter of Genesis, it was the corrupt inner nature of the offspring from these unions that caused God to regret that he had ever made humankind. For far more damaging than the physical merging of human and nonhuman forms was the merging in consciousness that these physical manifestations implied. Once again, souls were losing their awareness of their true spiritual nature, and consequently a great division arose between those souls who retained the awareness

of their oneness with God and those who had lost it.
Edgar Cayce referred to these two groups as the Sons of
the Law of One and the Sons of Belial, respectively, and
suggested that the first great earthly civilization, Atlantis, was built amidst this division.

The Edgar Cayce story of Atlantis is fascinating, rich
with significance for us today. For whether we regard it
as literal prehistoric fact or as one of the great myths
that touch the essence of human experience in the
earth, we find that it contains all of the great themes of
human existence: use of power, both material and spiritual; self-gratification versus self-transcendence; attunement to matter or attunement to spirit; affiliation with
others that builds cooperatively or aggression toward
others in the interests of self. We will not delve any
more deeply into the Atlantean legend, for that is a
book unto itself. We can, however, use what we have
seen of souls' earliest experiences in Atlantean civilization as a bridge to a more complete understanding of
the human condition, for we can readily recognize that
the central themes of Atlantean life are still central to
life today.

Atlantis eventually destroyed itself through misuse of
its spiritual and technological powers, but that was by no
means the end of earthly experience for the souls involved. With each subsequent civilization that has arisen
since that time, the experience of souls has been to
come in and out of earthly experience in order to grow
and learn and eventually remember who we really are.
Each lifetime (called a "sojourn" in the Cayce life readings) presents us with an opportunity to learn some specific lessons toward that end. Some of these lessons have
to do with overcoming undesirable patterns we have
built in our thoughts and in our actions, while others
have to do with enriching our experience and developing our nascent potential for love, creativity, and wisdom to its full maturity.

With each passing from physical life, when we leave behind the conscious mind that arises from material existence, we have the opportunity to review our progress and assess our soul growth needs from the deeper consciousness of nonphysical awareness. This is not to say that our disembodied consciousness is automatically in perfect touch with our deepest soul identity. Some of the self-created layers of distortion that we considered earlier cloud even our nonphysical state of awareness. But when we leave the physical body and the material consciousness that goes with it, we *are* that much closer to the core soul-identity and consequently we experience the potential for greater awareness of our true purpose as souls. In this heightened state of awareness following death, the soul takes stock of itself and recognizes where more development is needed. It is this awareness that draws us back into the earth when conditions are right for the next set of lessons.

In the meantime, we do not merely wait on the sidelines. Remember that from the beginning of our existence as individual souls the entire universe was our field of experience. This continues to be true. The earth holds the lessons that we can learn in a three-dimensional, material classroom, but there are still other planes of consciousness through which our souls pass in order to undergo other kinds of development. It is to these planes that we go in between earthly lives. Then, according to the growth needs of our soul, we come back into flesh existence to take up where we left off in our last incarnation.

Through it all, the love of our Creator and the law of cause and effect that flows from him guide us to a deeper understanding on the soul level of our experiences in materiality. The story of the soul in the earth thus far has been the story of a God who never ceases to give his children the opportunities they need in order to wake up to who they really are. It would be nice to carry that story on to its completion, but the last chapter is not yet ready to be told; we are writing it today and tomorrow with the choices we make.

4

TYING UP SOME LOOSE ENDS

Truth is growth! For what is truth today may be tomorrow only partially so, to a developing soul.
EDGAR CAYCE reading no. 1297–1

THE BASIC STORY OF reincarnation is deceptively simple. Fantastic though the epic story of souls in the earth may seem to some, the underlying concept of rebirth with its guiding law of cause and effect is so logical that it is easily understood even when it is not believed. For those who do embrace reincarnation as part of their personal beliefs, the very logic of the theory can lead to the assumption that the mysteries of the universe have been mastered. "Now I understand!" is frequently the inner response of those for whom the idea of reincarnation rings true.

But while the theory of reincarnation superbly addresses some of the most difficult questions concerning the meaning of life, it also leaves much still unanswered —or at least left to the realm of educated guessing. The old adage, "The more I know, the less I know," aptly describes what happens when we pursue some of the questions that arise with respect to the workings of reincarnation. For the deeper we go into an understanding of rebirth, the less we can afford to take the comfortable and complacent position that we have found all of the answers to life's riddles.

With this perspective serving as a disclaimer of sorts, let us address some of the most frequently asked questions regarding reincarnation. The responses I offer to these questions, as well as to those larger questions that are addressed with entire chapters later in this book, are not intended to be categorical pronouncements on The Way Things Are. Instead, they represent my best understanding of how these questions may be approached, using both the Edgar Cayce readings and the overall philosophy of reincarnation they suggest. The one thing I am certain of is this: however well we may think we understand the way life works, we're all going to be surprised when we reach a more enlightened state of consciousness and find out the truth. Like the people in Plato's parable of the cave, we are chained within the cavern of earthly awareness. Those glimpses we get of a higher reality are like shadows cast on the walls of our cave from the light above.

With this thought in mind, then, let's look at how we can reach at least a tentative understanding in response to some of the questions most frequently raised by the basic philosophy of reincarnation.

How Many Incarnations Does Each Soul Have?

Some thinkers on reincarnation have suggested that the number of lives any given soul may live in the earth is as great as the number of grains of sand on the beach. Such a concept defies our capacity to comprehend it; and, given the relatively short time that human life has existed on this globe, it seems to defy logic and history as well. We may be best off understanding the grains-of-sand analogy as a poetic expression of the long and varied history of every soul. This, certainly, is an understanding that is in accord with what the Cayce readings say about the soul's "sojourns" in the earth.

Cayce makes no specific statements concerning the number of lives allotted to each soul, but he does make it clear that those lives mentioned in any given life reading are merely a selection from a larger pool of past experiences. As he traces the history of a soul backward —from the twentieth century, to the French court of Louis XIV, to Rome under Caesar Augustus, to ancient Persia, and on to Atlantis, for example—it seems clear that these lives are mentioned because they relate directly to current-life patterns, opportunities, and difficulties, and not because they comprise the entirety of that soul's history. Furthermore, individuals who received subsequent life readings in follow-up to their original were told of additional past lives. The inference is that, as their development and understanding in this life grew, new relevancies to past experience emerged for these people. This is just one more indication that the lives Edgar Cayce singled out to discuss were just a portion of a much larger whole, with many more experiences left undiscussed and therefore undiscovered.

We can be fairly sure of one thing: the soul is given the opportunity for as many incarnations as it takes to accomplish its development. When we consider what a multifaceted task that is, and how long it takes the average person to overcome such common yet diverse human problems as overeating, phobias, or a tendency to gossip unkindly, we can begin to get some inkling of how many lives it takes to build up the wealth of experience necessary for full spiritual maturity. It is reasonable to assume, then, that we can number our lives in the hundreds and possibly even the thousands.

How Often Does the Soul Come Back to Earth?

Just as there is no standard number of lives for all souls, there is no set interval between lives. A soul may come back within weeks of its last death, or it may stay out of the earth plane for thousands of years. At least one person was told in his Cayce reading, for example, that he had not been in the earth since the time of Atlantis. This seems to be a rare circumstance, however; and we are probably safe in concluding that most of us return with far greater frequency.

The timing of any particular soul's reentry into a fleshly existence depends primarily on when conditions here on earth are such that the necessary lessons can be learned. The presence of certain other souls with whom an experience began in a past life is one example of the kind of condition that might bring a soul back to earth. Cultural or political climates may at times have to match those that existed when the soul had the earlier experience which led to the lesson now at hand. Sometimes sheer readiness to tackle a growth issue takes time, and so a soul will not enter physical life to deal with that issue until there is an inner readiness. All of this makes for considerable variation in between-life intervals, not only among different souls, but also in the experience of the same soul at different times.

When Does the Soul Enter the Body?

Here, too, there seems to be quite a bit of variation. In the majority of cases, the soul's entry seems to occur sometime near the time of birth, with the drawing of the first breath or just before or after that event. One way we can understand the lack of clarity we find in the readings on this question is to understand that entry may come in degrees rather than as an instant event. The Cayce readings tell us that the attitude of both parents at the time of conception has great influence on the selection of the soul that eventually enters, and that the mother's attitudes and habits especially have an influence on the traits of her unborn child. This information, along with some of the data suggested by hypnotic regressions to the months before birth, would indicate that there is some form of soul presence for much if not all of the gestation period. Even before the soul "enters" the body in the sense of fully incarnating, it may well be "hovering," so to speak—that is, present in consciousness to some extent as the development of the new body goes on within the mother.

Do We Only Come Back As Humans? Do Animals Have Souls?

The Cayce readings indicate that our experience in incarnation is limited to the human form. With the exception of those early experiences we considered in the last chapter, when souls of their own accord merged themselves with aspects of the animal world, animal incarnations are not a part of the experience of the soul in the earth. The broader theory of transmigration, which includes the possibility of incarnations in other life forms alternately with human experiences, did not seem to be embraced in the life readings.

Animals, as living beings, possess spirit; but they are not fully individuated souls consisting of spirit, mind, and will. The readings do not address this question at great length, but there is some vague indication that animal spirit may nonetheless participate in the continuity of life. A reading that told a woman that her pet cat had been with her in another life in Egypt provokes speculation on this possibility. The answer may lie in the concept of our souls' capacity to create thought forms; that is, with the creative patterning aspects of our minds, we may create the thought form of our pets' "individuality" out of the basic animal spirit they possess. Thus, while all animals are animated by the life force we call spirit, some animals may take on a human-created individuality of sorts that involves them in something more closely resembling our process of reincarnation.

Do Heaven, Hell, and Purgatory Fit into the Philosophy of Reincarnation?

Heaven is described in the Cayce readings as being in the presence of God; hell is separation from God. Both states are built by the soul. We may experience heaven in moments of spiritual ecstasy, and we may experience hell in times of anguish. Both of these states may be experienced while we are here in a physical body, or they may be a state of consciousness that we experience in the between-life state.

The separation and torment we can experience between lives as a result of our own negative thought creations is analogous to purgatory. Because one can get caught in this state of consciousness and think it is permanent, the Cayce readings encouraged us to pray for those who have made their transition from material life. Our prayers can help those who might be caught in self-created darkness wake up and move on to their next stage of development.

In ultimate terms, heaven is the state we will be in when we have reached our full maturity as companions and cocreators with God. Hell, in the final sense of absolute and permanent separation from God, is a state that God will never inflict on any soul. Each soul will have as many opportunities as it takes to return to full consciousness of oneness with God. But, because we do have free will, the readings also say that the soul has the freedom to "banish itself" from God's presence. Thus hell does have reality in ultimate as well as temporal terms.

If All Souls Were Created "Before the Beginning," How Do We Explain Population Growth?

Undeniably, the number of people on earth has grown. There have been a few dips along the way, but generally speaking the population has steadily increased. Where are the additional souls coming from?

The answer to this question probably lies in remembering that the earth is not the only plane of existence for souls. As we have already seen, there are other levels of experience that the soul goes to when it is not in the earth. Students at a large university, for example, might attend the college of law, the college of education, the college of fine arts, and so on. By analogy, those souls who are in the earth plane at any given time do not represent the entire "student population" of the universe, but rather those souls who are enrolled in "College Earth." At any given time in the earth's history, it is likely that only a relatively small percentage of the total number of souls have been here at one time. Enrollment in College Earth may currently be at an all-time high, and this suggests that events and circumstances here are such that learning opportunities for souls are abundant right now. But even now, with so many souls in the earth, there are probably more souls *not* in the earth than there are *in* physical form.

Is There Any Connection Between Reincarnation and Astrology?

The Cayce readings indicate a strong connection. Not only did the first reference to reincarnation arise from a reading that requested a horoscope, but the life readings given thereafter began with a detailed discussion of astrological aspects at birth. Some of this data presents a real puzzle for astrologers, however, because it does not seem totally consistent with any established school of astrology.

In the scheme suggested by the life readings, these aspects can best be understood in terms of the between-life experiences in other planes of consciousness. The planets of our solar system, which figure so prominently in astrology, represent the other dimensions of consciousness that we go to after we leave an earthly life, according to Cayce. The experiences in a given life influence where our soul "goes" in its post-death journey to another state of consciousness. That state of consciousness is in turn reflected in the natal chart whenever the soul returns to earth. Thus the astrological aspects discussed by Cayce were closely connected with past-life influences.

The readings were emphatic on the point that the influences reflected in a natal chart were only a picture of the potentials arising from the soul's past experiences, and did not predetermine us to any particular destiny. Consistent with the worldview expressed elsewhere in the readings, the readings that discussed astrological aspects insisted that will had supreme power over all such influences.

Is Reincarnation an Anti-Christian Philosophy?

Reincarnation, as a general philosophy, is neither Christian nor anti-Christian. Because of its strong emphasis on the spiritual nature of humanity and its relationship to God, there are obvious religious connotations that lead some people to consider it a distinct religion that stands in contrast to another religion such as Christianity. Actually, though, reincarnation is not a religion, but a philosophy that may be incorporated into many different religious persuasions. Thus one may be a reincarnationist and also be a Christian,* Jew, Hindu, Buddhist, and so on.

What Is Group Karma?

Just as individual souls come in and out of the earth in order to learn specific things necessary to their development, groups of souls tend to come in and out of the earth together as they learn similar lessons. These groups may be relatively small—a handful of souls working out the complexities of their interrelationships through a series of lives in which the roles of parent, child, husband, wife, brother, and sister are interchangeable from one experience to the next, for example. They may be larger, as in the case of what the readings refer to as "national karma," where a group of souls works through its common experience under the banner of a particular nationality. Soul groups are bonded according to similar values, too, as we find indicated in readings that talk of a group of souls entering incarnation whose primary concern would be materialism.

Some of the most interesting group karma mentioned in the readings concerned groups of souls who were coming into the earth now because of some common experience in an earlier epoch, such as Atlantis or Egypt. The years 1910 and 1911 were mentioned specifically as being years that brought a great influx of Atlantean souls. Given what the readings suggest about the

* While it is beyond the scope of this present work to address the special concerns of Christians regarding the law of karma and the Christian belief that Jesus atoned for our sins when he died on the cross, these issues are addressed in some depth in my book *Edgar Cayce and the Born Again Christian*. However, one aspect of this issue that we will address later in this book comes up in chapter thirteen, which deals with the law of grace and what Edgar Cayce called the Christ consciousness.

technological advancement of Atlantis, it is interesting to note the great technological leaps forward that took place in our century as those born in 1910 and 1911 reached adulthood.

In another intriguing reference to group karma, the readings predicted that the souls entering the earth from 1943 through 1945 would "fulfill interesting roles in their service to their fellow man, finding a very unusual approach to same." When we project that soul group ahead to their young adulthood, we find ourselves considering the mid-1960s, certainly a time when much of a generation took an unusual approach to "service to their fellow man."

Group karma is not, however, an indissoluble bond that all participants must endure whether they like it or not. The only thing that binds us to other souls is our continuing to hold in our consciousness (or, more specifically, unconsciousness) the memories and values that the group shares. We are part of a group's karma only so long as we continue to hold whatever that group's karma may be as our *personal* karma as well. As we will see in our later consideration of grace, the choice to hold on to or let go of karma truly is ours to make.

What About Soul Mates and Twin Souls?

These special relationships between two souls are really just one-on-one versions of the same dynamic we have just considered in relation to group karma. Soul mates are those souls with whom we have forged close bonds through a series of harmonious life experiences together. Thus it is entirely possible and even probable that any given person has more than one soul mate.

Twin souls seem to derive their connectedness to one another from a common bond on the level of mind, rather than because of earthly lives lived together. This bond may have to do with that initial process of polarizing male and female, which was discussed in the last chapter. While I must emphasize again that the Cayce readings were not entirely clear on this point, it seems that a pairing of sorts occurred as some souls polarized toward the male aspect and others polarized toward the female. Adam and Eve were twin souls, for example, and so were Jesus and his mother, Mary, according to Cayce. Since the soul's occupation of a physical body can and does shift back and forth between the two sexes, twin souls will not always find themselves in bodies of opposite sexes; sometimes they may be of the same sex. The element of the original pairing of souls that apparently endures as the common bond between twin souls is a common ideal or purpose.

With neither soul mates nor twin souls do both participants in the relationship have to be incarnate at the same time. Even when they are, it may or may not be best for their development to be together in any given life. The harmonious communion between soul mates may in some cases be conducive to growth, but at other times the growth that comes through the struggles of a more problematic relationship may be more to the point. Similarly, the commonality of purpose on a mental level between twin souls may in some cases bring needed strength to both parties when they are able to work at life together, while in other contexts it would be a superfluous duplication of effort.

What About Parallel Lives and Walk-ins?

The Cayce readings do not mention either parallel lives (the concept that one soul may incarnate in two or more human bodies simultaneously) or "walk-ins" (souls who incarnate into a body that is voluntarily surrendered by its previous soul-inhabitant). This may be because these situations do not occur, or it may be because they would not have been meaningful concepts at the time or to the people whom Edgar Cayce was addressing. In either case, it is important to keep in mind that our understanding is always going to be limited by the earthly dimension in which we live. Any systems we devise for understanding the ultimate realities of life should be seen as partial understandings at best.

The system developed in the Cayce readings suggests a somewhat linear experience within the earth plane: one soul moving through one body at a time in synchronization with the natural cycles of birth and death. Under this system, we may understand experiences that seem to suggest that two people have a common soul as arising from the underlying oneness among *all* souls; that is, even though we are individuals, we are also part of a larger whole. When two people experience the intensity of connection and similarity of experience and makeup that might indicate "parallel lives," they may in fact be experiencing the oneness that characterizes all existence, but which is so seldom actually felt.

Similarly, the apparent changes of soul within a given physical life, which lead to the walk-in theory, may be due to the soul's many-faceted nature. Each one of us is comprised of many selves, built over many life experiences. At any given time, we are showing and identifying with just a few small aspects of our total makeup. The shifts in priorities and values and even lifestyle that signal the presence of a walk-in, according to some points of view, may instead be a signal that the individual has moved into another phase of its own experience and identity.

If Souls Are Growing and Developing Through Their Incarnations, Why Is the World Still in Such a Mess?

It is easy enough to see why this question comes up frequently when people consider the hypothesis of reincarnation. War, greed, selfishness and every form of atrocity imaginable are going on in this world every day. Even when we survey individual lives—our own, or those of the people closest to us—it is clear that the qualities we would associate with being a companion to God are still beyond our attainment. After all of these thousands of years of earthly life, shouldn't we be getting better?

The answer to that question, if we stop and think about it, is that we really *are* getting better. We might not see the kind of forward stride that we would ideally like to see, but our collective sense of conscience and decency are in truth becoming more acute, as we can see when we compare prevailing standards in the world today against those of earlier times. For example, it was relatively recently (by earth-history standards) that people would gather in a colosseum to watch other human beings be torn apart by lions—and call it entertainment. Certainly not everyone in the Roman Empire condoned such "sport," but it was acceptable by societal standards. Today it would be the misfit and not the member of mainstream society who would even contemplate such atrocity as a form of entertainment. In other words, even though it is true that terrible acts of violence and hate still take place in this world every day, such acts are more frequently recognized as wrong, and fewer people willingly participate in them. Moreover, slavery, once common to every continent, has disappeared from the face of the earth. There is a discernible shifting of val-

ues, even though it might not be as complete as we
would wish.

In order to understand the seeming snail's pace at
which our collective development manifests in the
world, we must keep in mind what we have seen in the
preceding two chapters about the creations of the mind.
All of the patterning and shaping of reality that we engage in takes place first on the mental and spiritual
levels. That means that soul development starts there as
well. It is only as the final step of the creation process
that our mental patterns manifest in the material level
of reality. Thus our development—both individual and
collective—takes place first on the level of internal reality. Only later can it be seen in the physical world. This
means that there is a delayed reaction between the development that we experience on the soul level and the
manifestation of that development in material life.

When Do We Know That We Are Finished with Our Development and Do Not Have to Come Back?

Some people were told in their Cayce life readings that
if they continued living their lives as they had been con-
ducting them up to that point, they would have the option of not reincarnating. To be more specific, eighteen
out of the approximately 1,500 individuals who had life
readings were told this. However, we cannot look to
these cases for a portrait of "the soul who has completed its development," for they are a varied group.
Their soul histories and their current-life circumstances
did not follow any recognizable pattern. Their lives even
had an assortment of the kind of troubles and frustra-
tions that plague most of us. The one thing they did
seem to have in common was an orientation toward service to others.

These people had not reached perfection, but they had apparently completed the lessons that the earth plane has to offer. We can infer that there were other lessons in other planes of consciousness still left for them to learn, and it was made quite clear in their readings that the option to return to earth if they chose to would be open to them.

If we are to learn anything from these eighteen people concerning the question of when any given soul no longer has to come back, perhaps the most significant clue lies in the fact that none of these individuals had *asked* Cayce to tell them when they would be done with their earthly development. For to ask when we will no longer have to come back to earthly life is one of those interesting questions that carries its own answer within itself: as long as we are hoping to hear that we will not have to reincarnate, we can be reasonably sure that we *will* have to return. The soul who experiences life as a burden to be lifted at the earliest possible opportunity is a soul who has not yet learned what it means to experience the beauty and goodness of the created world without becoming enslaved by it.

A story from the Buddhist tradition illustrates this point: Two disciples are praying in the woods when the master appears. One looks up from his meditation and asks, "Master, how many more lives do I have to live before I reach enlightenment?" "Only three more, my son," is the master's response. "Three more lives . . ." the discouraged disciple repeats to himself; and he goes back to his meditation. Meanwhile, the second disciple comes dancing up to his master asking the same question. "How many more lives do I have to live?" "One thousand more, I'm afraid, my son," is the grave response. "A thousand more!" the disciple exclaims in glee as he goes dancing off into the woods. And instantly he becomes enlightened.

Part II

LESSONS IN THE SCHOOL OF LIFE

For each entity in the earth is what it is because of what it has been! And each moment is dependent upon another moment. So a sojourn in the earth, as indicated, is as a lesson in the school of life and experience. Just as it may be illustrated in that each entity, each soul-entity, is as a corpuscle in the body of God—if such an entity has applied itself in such a manner as to be a helpful force and not a rebellious force.

EDGAR CAYCE reading no. 2823–3

5

LEARNING AND GROWING THROUGH CAUSE AND EFFECT

Thus we find, as in this entity's experiences, those influences that bring again, again, again, the opportunity to know the Lord that He IS good.

EDGAR CAYCE reading no. 1215–4

NOW THAT WE HAVE examined the essential elements of the philosophy of reincarnation and what it suggests about the nature of life, the soul, and our reason for returning to the earth again and again, let's take that exploration to a far more personal level. For reincarnation *is* an intensely personal philosophy. It is personal in the sense that the individual theoretical concepts that make up the overall philosophy have the potential to revolutionize not only the way we *look* at life's experiences, but the way we *experience* them.

From the moment we begin to understand *what* reincarnation is and *why* we are here in this life, changes start to take place in the way we "process" the things that happen to us day by day; that is, we fit our daily experiences into a different framework of reality and we choose and evaluate our responses to people and circumstances according to a different understanding. This is why "discovering" reincarnation is for so many people a transformative experience.

The next six chapters will deal with this transformative experience in greater detail, concentrating on how reincarnation works in our lives. We'll begin in this chapter with an examination of how an understanding of karma can change our entire outlook on life. In chapter six we'll see how karma not only helps us make the very most of the opportunities in our lives, but also turns problem situations and painful experiences into positive growth experiences. In subsequent chapters we will consider how the soul thinks and chooses; and how, when, and why we are drawn into a particular body, a unique set of family relationships, and an environment that best suits our soul's needs. We'll also look at past-life memory. Can we remember? Is remembering a good idea? How can we use past-life memories when they do come?

Let's begin, then, to explore the life-changing nature of the philosophy of reincarnation by taking a closer look at what an understanding of the law of karma (or cause and effect) does to our thinking.

OUR RELATIONSHIP TO THE UNIVERSE

A Sense of Control

When we accept the law of cause and effect, we bring a sense of predictability and control into our lives. The law of karma tells us that life is not a series of random events. We are not victims when things go wrong. We are not "lucky" when they go right. We are free, choosing agents, souls living within an orderly system that promises us a predictable link between the choices we make and the experiences that ensue.

This conviction that we are in control challenges us to create positive conditions in our lives wherever possible. It is not enough to sit back and hope for things to turn out right. To allow ourselves to be guided by circumstances, taking a "hit or miss" approach to life, was specifically discouraged in the Cayce readings because such passivity denies our selfhood. Nor is it growth-promoting to abdicate our freedom of choice to another person. Time and time again people tried in vain to get Edgar Cayce to tell them what to do. "Should I marry this person?" "Should I take this job or the other one?" "Where should I live?" These were typical questions, and many of us would love to have them answered today. Yet Cayce was adamant in his refusal to do other people's choosing for them. He might have pointed out the issues that they ought to keep in mind as they chose, but always he reminded them that the choice itself would best come from what the individual found to be most in keeping with his or her desires *and* innermost ideals.

Perhaps the ultimate statement from Cayce concerning our power to choose our circumstances came when he was asked, "Is there likelihood of bad health in March?" His wry response: "If you are looking for it, you can have it in February. If you want to skip March, skip it, you'll have it in June. If you want to skip June, don't have it at all this year!" Yes, the law of karma challenges us to seize every opportunity to choose the very best for our lives. It leaves us no option to coast through life, for it insists that we are always choosing. To quote the popular poster message of the 1970s, "Not to decide is to decide." The law of karma promises us that we always have the option of choosing in ways that *must* —according to law—bring the very best into our lives.

Acceptance of the law of karma also works wonders in giving us the gumption and endurance it sometimes takes to get through life's difficult times. This is because endurance tends to run in direct proportion to our sense of control over the circumstance being endured. I had an early experience with this important principle when I made my first childhood trip to the dentist. I had heard other children talk about the traumas of dental work, so it was with a certain amount of trepidation that I sat in the chair and allowed the assistant to clip the bib around my neck. After the examination, my worst fears were confirmed: the dentist told me that he would have to fill a cavity. Ironically, my fear of the needle that would administer Novocaine was far greater than my fear of the drill. And so the dentist, with a creative insight that only became apparent to me in later years, suggested that we go ahead without the Novocaine. The arms of my chair were connected with his drill, he told me. All I had to do was squeeze the arms of the chair whenever the drilling became uncomfortable, and this would automatically stop his drill.

Confident that I had control over what was about to happen, and relieved that I would not have to face the needle after all, I was only too happy to go along with this plan. Sure enough, every time a twinge of pain led me to squeeze the arms of the chair, the drill would slow down and stop. As soon as I relaxed my grip, it would pick up again. The sense that I could stop the pain of the drilling with just the squeeze of my hands gave me a sense of mastery over it. And with that sense of mastery came the willingness to endure the twinges just a little bit longer before stopping the drill. After all, the fewer the interruptions, the sooner the tooth would be filled and I would be on my way home again.

It was years before I realized that the only connection between the arms of that chair and the action of the drill was my dentist's careful observation of my response as he worked. In the meantime, I had developed the ability to sit through an entire filling without having to shut the drill off once! What's more, I had developed none of the fear of going to the dentist that plagues so many people.

I have come to see this early experience with a very wise dentist as an allegory of how an understanding of the law of cause and effect helps us endure and even master the painful experiences in life. Nothing exacerbates pain more than the sense of helplessness. Feeling out of control, never knowing whether the pain is going to reach proportions that are beyond endurance, and anticipating the worst can make even minimal pain seem unbearable. This applies not only to physical pain, but to emotional, mental, and spiritual anguish as well.

Herein lies one of the great transformative secrets of the philosophy of reincarnation. For with the law of cause and effect in our thinking, we have the assurance that we really *are* in control of our fates—even when it doesn't seem like it. With an understanding of the law of karma, we know the rules of the game and can therefore play our hand in a winning fashion. And there is the added realization that, even before we consciously learned those rules, our deeper selves have been working within their framework. Therefore *all* of our experiences are the product of our own choices, both conscious and unconscious; and in a very real sense, nothing happens to us without our soul's cooperation and permission. The spouse who mistreats us, the child who disappoints us, the money problems that challenge us—all of these things are allowed to enter our lives only as our deepest self recognizes the growth opportunities they provide. Not only does this realization give us the sense that our difficulties fall within our own control, but it assures us that even life's greatest upheavals can move us toward harmony with our soul's deepest purpose.

The knowledge that there are reliable laws in this universe, that we already know them on a soul level, and that we are fully capable of learning and working with them on a conscious level has to do with affirming the ultimate harmony and orderliness of this universe. This, too, as we shall see, is one of the transformative aspects of the philosophy of reincarnation. For when we acknowledge the law of karma as a working principle in our lives, we are acknowledging a profound connectedness with all of reality.

The Ultimate Harmony of the Universe

The law of cause and effect aligns us with the ultimate harmony of the universe. When we incorporate into our thinking a law of cause and effect that governs events in our lives, determines the people who will participate in our experience, and orchestrates the things that happen to us as we unfold, we begin to live with the conviction that there is a meaningful order to all that happens, that the law of karma works only to promote our own ultimate well-being. Then the spiritual path is not a way of drudgery. It does not consist of the performance of unpleasant, albeit necessary, duties. It carries instead a promise of greater harmony with what genuinely feels good.

I do not mean to imply that cooperation with the law is effortless or that, "If it feels good, it must be right." Of course it may take effort at times to think and speak and act in ways that are in keeping with your soul's deepest ideals. There are bound to be times when the choice of greatest *immediate* appeal is that of "me first," even at the cost of others' good. We all face crossroads where short-term gratification lies down the road of selfishness, dishonesty, laziness, vengefulness, or any of a number of human vices. And at times it will not be easy to choose a direction opposite the one that promises gratification in the short term. In this sense, the "right" choices are at times *hard* choices. But when we approach life from the perspective that karma moves us into greater harmony with the ultimate harmony of the universe, we realize that what is "right" and what brings happiness are actually the same thing.

The crucial point here is that right living and thinking

(and its resultant well-being) have their origin in the oneness between God and each soul he has created. The "right" way of living and thinking isn't right because God decided it was right; it is right because it *is* God, it flows from God's very nature. To state it another way, karmic law is not an arbitrary code of behavior; it is an expression of the ultimate unity, harmony, and *goodness* of the universe. We have already seen that karma is nothing more than the universe maintaining harmony within itself. Any action or thought that is in harmony with the unified goodness of the universe multiplies into more harmony and goodness. Any action or thought that is not in harmony with the unified goodness of the universe will necessarily set up discord. When we experience the manifestations of our inharmonious choices, we say we are meeting a "karmic debt"; in reality, we are merely receiving feedback that tells us we've moved out of harmony with the deeper good that is the only source of true happiness.

More than semantics is at stake when we distinguish between law as a code of behavior established *by* God, and law as an expression *of* God. As long as we see the "right" answers to life's choices as being selected and then enforced by someone outside of ourselves—even if that someone is God himself—we are externally motivated in our attempts to obey those laws. An externally imposed law stands as a reminder of our separation from the lawmaker, or God. We may try to obey that law willingly, out of love for God. We may do it begrudgingly as the only way to "make it" in the system. Or we may not try to obey at all, instead rebelling against the law and bearing the consequences in a resentful and self-destructive frame of mind. Chances are, we do a little of each at various times in our lives. But whichever mode of response we take to the externally generated law, we are missing out on one of the great transformative secrets in the philosophy of reincarnation: the law of karma is an expression of the essential connectedness between God and humankind, and as such it is a law that emphasizes oneness between Creator and creature rather than separation or rebellion. It is the expression of an ultimate reality that is, by its very nature, good. In the next chapter we will focus on the specific ways this law operates in our lives.

6

HOW THE LAW OF KARMA
WORKS IN DAILY EXPERIENCE

*For one enters a material sojourn not by chance,
but there is brought into being the continuity of
pattern or purpose, and each soul is attracted to
the influences which may be visions from above.
Thus there the turns in the river of life may be
viewed. To be sure, there are floods in the life;
there are dark days and there are days of sunshine.
But the soul-entity stayed in a purpose that is
creative, even as this entity may find the haven of
peace which is declared in Him.*

EDGAR CAYCE reading no. 3128–1

IT IS IMPORTANT THAT we know as much as possible about the way the law of karma expresses itself in our daily lives. Although it is helpful just to realize that the law of cause and effect is operative in all of our experience, the more we learn to recognize specific instances of karma in action, the better equipped we are to learn quickly from it. If we can learn to trace specific causes—which we set in motion in our lives—to the effects they bring, we are better able to recognize and choose constructive causes, and we are better able to understand and cope with painful effects when they do occur.

Superficially, the law of cause and effect is very cut and dried: for every cause there is an effect, for every action there is a reaction. The simple logic of these statements can lull us into thinking that karma is a very easy matter to understand. But most "simple" spiritual truths have the capacity to unfold into endless varieties of expression in material existence. The law of cause and effect is no exception to this rule.

Suppose, for example, that you have gone through this life yearning for riches. Your dreams consist of Rolls Royces and jewels and furs. You spend your whole life wishing you could have those things, yet they never come your way. The law of karma tells you that this yearning has its origins in a prior life. Just what are these circumstances and traits saying about your past life? Perhaps in another life you had great wealth, so in this life you still want wealth. Maybe you misused that wealth and that's why you can't have it again. On the other hand, the current situation may be the result of another life in which you were a pauper. In this life you still find yourself yearning for riches beyond what you will actually achieve.

In the example above we see two very different past lives that could, with equal logic, be used to explain a present-day situation. Typically, a single current-life situation can be explained in two or more ways according to the law of karma. This is an important point, because our capacity consciously to assimilate the lessons of karma will usually depend upon our being able to entertain several possible karmic explanations for our circumstances.

Fortunately, the multitudinous variety of ways that cause and effect might express itself tend to fall into a few basic categories that we can use to understand how karma interacts with our own choices. What follows, then, is a discussion of four of the main pathways that the law of cause and effect may take as it leads us along from one lifetime to the next—or as it leads us through the experiences of a single lifetime, for that matter.

THE LAW OF CONTINUATION

One of the clearest ways to illustrate the action of the law of cause and effect within our soul experience is to observe its physical action in the material world. For example, the karmic action that we are going to call the *law of continuation* is best understood if we think about what happens when we throw a ball out into an open airspace. It is logical to expect that the ball will continue traveling in the direction in which it was thrown—until gravity pulls it down or until it hits some obstacle. This same principle, when applied to our personal experiences, suggests that there is a tendency for our actions, our choices, and our traits to have a momentum that continues from lifetime to lifetime. This means that our biases, tastes, relationships, and efforts all tend to be continued or carried on from one lifetime to another.

The karmic law of continuation contains the good news that no effort is ever lost. It says that you can spend most of your life struggling at a problem relationship, and even if you don't quite get it perfect, you will come into your next lifetime with the effect of all of that good effort working for you in relationships. The law of continuation is the law that says you can work very hard to become proficient with an artistic ability, never reach excellence, and yet come into the next lifetime with all of that practice already there for you to draw upon.

However, the effects of the causes we set in motion are temporary in the sense that a direction started will not continue forever without additional thrust behind it. Gravity will pull any ball to the ground sooner or later, depending on how hard it is thrown. A half-hearted throw wouldn't send the ball very far. Similarly, our life direction, attitudes, and efforts will only carry us as far as the energy we put into them allows. We must keep those positive forces active through repeated practice.

The law of continuation reflects the other side of the coin as well. Our favorite prejudices and cherished biases will carry a momentum beyond this life. If nothing comes along to change them, they will manifest anew in the next experience on earth. Enlightenment does not come over us magically at death, erasing all of our shortcomings. Nor do we routinely give up our individualized viewpoints for some universal truth. Cayce illustrates this point rather colorfully when he says, "For do not consider for a moment . . . than an individual soul-entity passing from an earth plane as a Catholic, a Methodist, an Episcopalian, is something else just because he is dead! He's only a dead Episcopalian, Catholic, or Methodist" (no. 254–92). The karmic law of cause and effect, when it takes a path of continuation, reflects our tendency to carry on in a new setting and under new circumstances pretty much the same old things.

Just as our positive life directions are kept energized through repeated choice, the negative forces are kept alive chiefly in the same way—through allowing them to become ingrained in our ways of thinking and living, to the point where we keep creating our negative and limiting patterns anew.

If the law of continuation were the only way that karma worked, our negative and destructive pattern could come to an end in one way only: when we ceased to put energy behind them. Yet many of these patterns, by their very nature, blind us to the awareness that what we are doing *is* destructive. The self-delusion and the blunting of conscience that tell us we need not change are part and parcel of most of our destructive patterns. Just as it is most difficult for the alcoholic or the drug addict to recognize the presence of an addiction and its destructive nature, we are least able to recognize our addictions to destructive patterns of outlook, habit, or behavior when we are caught in the midst of them. The prognosis for the human soul would be poor indeed if spontaneous awakening to our destructive ways were our only means of discovering we were going the wrong way.

Fortunately for us, our destructive thoughts and actions, precisely because they *do* create discord within a universe that *must*, according to its very nature, maintain harmony, become the seeds of an opposing force that will push us back toward harmony. This brings us to a consideration of the next pathway that karma can take.

THE LAW OF CONSEQUENCES

To continue our analogy from material experience, even the ball thrown out with the strongest of thrusts will, theoretically, hit some obstacle eventually. If a person had the superhuman strength to throw a ball that traveled for miles, that ball would still eventually hit a wall or a fence or some obstacle. Just so, even the negative thought or behavior pattern that is kept energized by continual feeding and repetition will create a "psychic wall" of discord, as we have seen. When our physical ball hits a wall, it bounces back toward the thrower. When our thoughts and actions hit their psychic wall, they bounce back to us like a boomerang. Our chickens come home to roost. This is the *law of consequences.*

Consider, for example, the woman who came to Edgar Cayce for a reading because she was having a very disappointing love life. Time after time, her heart was broken. Her reading traced this unhappy pattern back to a prior life in which she had had many suitors, and had been very superficial in her approach to them. She had allowed them to lose their hearts to her and encouraged their affections. Once they were in love with her, she would spurn them and go on to the next one.

The law of continuation would tell us that this soul

would carry similar attitudes toward lovers in this life.
Yet instead of continuing to break hearts, she is now
experiencing what it is like to have her heart broken.
What happened here? What brought about the transition that ended the perpetuation of a pattern of undesirable behavior and brought on this soul's experience
with the consequence of that behavior? Apparently, this
soul hit the "psychic wall" of discord created by her
behavior and is now "bouncing" back toward harmony.

In order to understand this transition, it may help to
remember the concept of the soul taking stock of itself
between lifetimes. In the after-death state, a soul seems
to have the potential to "wake up"; that is, to recognize
violations of its own ideals or, to put it another way,
become aware of the discord its acts in the body have
created. The moment when this takes place is the
psychic equivalent of the ball hitting a wall. Then the
consequences come.

The law of consequences can provide some of the
most dramatic examples in the literature of reincarnation, for it is under the workings of this law that we find
people "meeting their karma" through great hardship,
life tragedies, and handicaps. That central premise of
ancient law, "An eye for an eye, a tooth for a tooth," is
carried out even if it takes more than the span of one
lifetime to accomplish. One Edgar Cayce life reading
attributed a man's congenital blindness to an experience
in ancient Persia, in which he had blinded his enemies
with hot pokers. Another man's deafness was linked to a
prior life in which he had repeatedly "turned a deaf
ear" to those in need.

Karmic consequences can also take physical forms of
less magnitude than major handicaps. Often people
were told in their Cayce readings that their physical ailments were the consequence of past-life habits, choices,
or values. One man's gastrointestinal problems were
traced to a previous life as a glutton; another's sterility

to past-life sexual excesses. Even seemingly minor afflictions may have karmic implications. Consider the present-day case of a woman with an extreme allergic sensitivity to the sun. Her personal past-life exploration led her to recall a life among people who valued white, untanned skin as a sign of genteel social class.

It is important to bear in mind, however, that the law of consequences is not the only explanation for life's adversities. Every time we see someone suffering a hardship, living with a handicap, or facing a tragedy, we should not assume that that soul is experiencing a karmic lesson or meeting the consequence of one of its own destructive choices in the past. Sometimes the soul takes on conditions of adversity or handicap not because it is meeting the law of consequences, but because in one way or another this choice represents an act of service or an exercise in accelerated growth.

For example, a soul may come in with a handicap such as blindness in order to help others who are blind. A soul may be born into poverty in order to serve the poor as one who lives among them day by day. A child who lives a brief and sickly life may have come more for the sake of helping the parents learn some part of their soul-growth lessons than because of its own growth needs. The opposite may be true as well: the heartbreak of caring for a sick child may be a burden voluntarily taken on by the parents as an act of service toward a soul who is going through a difficult lesson. In other words, we can never judge from the outside looking in and automatically assume that someone is meeting karma just because he or she faces adversity.

There is also the possibility that souls can take on very difficult circumstances for the purpose of flexing their spiritual muscles—the metaphysical version of "no pain, no gain." They take on hard life conditions because this is where the greatest opportunity for growth can be. Voluntarily tackling difficult life circumstances is akin to the way some students choose their courses in school. When students are given the freedom to select some of their classes, some will say, "I want to get through with as little sweat as possible," and they will take the easiest courses available and seek out the least demanding teachers. Other students will say, "I want to learn as much as I can while I'm here," and they'll sign on for some tough courses. Sometimes the students in the easy classes get better grades than those in the more demanding courses; but the real question is, which students are learning more? Does an A in an easy course reflect as much enrichment as a C in a difficult course? Just so, we as souls gain or lose in our life experiences based on whether they enlarge us, not on whether they appear smooth and easy to an onlooker.

It may be very important, then, to temper our understanding of the law of consequences with the knowledge that it is only *one* explanation for life's difficulties. Certainly, when we face adversity in our lives, it is good and healthy to stop and ask ourselves whether the trouble is evidence of the law of consequences in action. To be able to entertain the possibility that we have created our problems in the past is a good sign. It indicates that we are indeed growing up spiritually and learning to take responsibility for our lives. At the same time, however, it can be unhealthy to let the law of consequences so dominate your thinking that it leads to never-ending guilt.

If, every time something goes wrong, your first response is to beat your breast and ask, "What have I done to deserve this?" (and the question is not rhetorical—you really believe you have brought it on yourself), it may be time to stop and consider the possibility that you are missing the point. You may well have taken the difficulty on for the growth it offers you. More important still, when the law of consequences leads us to look at the adversities of other people and dispassionately conclude that they must be getting what they deserve from a karmic perspective, it becomes nothing more than an excuse for self-centered complacency. Such thinking will surely lead to karmic consequences of its own.

THE LAW OF POSITIVE RETURN

Lest we lose sight of the positive effects that come to us from our positive actions (so-called "good karma"), we must keep in mind that there are also karmic consequences to the acts of kindness, compassion, and service that we perform. We will call this principle the *law of positive return.*

This law is similar to the law of continuation, in that it brings to us in subsequent lives (or later on in this one) the fruits of our good efforts. It is different, because the effects we experience go far beyond the original investment we made. We may draw the distinction in this way: where continuation inclines us to perpetuate the original good choices and actions, positive return enables us to reap the multiplied benefits of those choices. It is analogous to a bank savings account. Each deposit will add to a balance that is always there for the depositor to draw upon; that is like the workings of the law of continuation. By contrast, the interest the account earns causes the balance to *multiply.* This is like the good that returns to us manyfold through the law of karma. The bank is able to make interest payments on a savings account because it has used the depositor's money to earn even more money in other transactions. Similarly, our good actions send a force out into the world that multiplies, creating even more good than we were originally capable of. From that abundance of good, dividends return to us.

For example, the person blessed with a body that

seems naturally prone toward robust good health may
be experiencing the consequences of a life spent bringing health to the sick bodies of others. The person who
seems to breeze along with a good marriage, well-ad-
justed kids, and a tranquil home life may have worked
very hard in a past life to bring peace and tranquility
into the lives of others. The person with the Midas
touch, where every investment brings great return, every
job holds a good salary, and money seems to flow abun-
dantly, may be reaping the consequences of great generosity in a prior life.

Because of the law of positive return, we can expect
someday to find ourselves the beneficiary of positive actions and choices much like the ones we have the opportunity to make right now. We can know that we are
creating future conditions for ourselves similar to the
conditions others will experience as a result of our
choices today. Such knowledge may at times make the
difference between a choice for selfishness and a choice
for love, kindness, or generosity.

For the person of acute conscience, this promise of
multiplied return for our good poses a moral dilemma.
Doesn't the expectation of return taint the original
goodness? An old adage tells us that virtue is its own
reward. Anyone who has ever felt the inner glow that
comes from a secret act of kindness or generosity will
know that this is true. But doesn't even this inner glow
become an expected return for good deeds? Indeed, it
may be argued that no act of charity is ever free of
selfishness, as even that glow of satisfaction or the freedom from guilt that results from our good deeds is a
reward. Admittedly, the hope of return is not the most
noble motive for making positive, constructive choices
in life. But some consciousness of benefit to ourselves
seems unavoidable; and a clear sense of the promised
reward sure can help at times.

In an ideal world, our acts of goodness will flow from

sheer love for one another and for God. But in the meantime, most of us will find if we are honest with ourselves that there are times when we must consciously choose goodness in the face of temptation to do otherwise. At those times, the added incentive that comes from knowing that our attempts at virtue, however imperfect, will not be in vain can help us to make the choice that will fortify us and take us that much closer to the day when we can consistently choose goodness out of pure love.

THE LAW OF BALANCE

Sometimes the law of cause and effect will bounce us from one extreme to another. This is because at times we need to experience extremes in order to find the appropriate middle ground. When we become so identified with one side of human experience that we are seemingly unable even to know about the reality of the other side, a lifetime in the exact opposite circumstance may come along to shake us out of our lopsidedness. This is the *law of balance*.

For example, a lifetime of extreme shyness may lead to a compensating lifetime with a very aggressive nature. From the two extremes, the best aspects of meekness and the best of aggression can be combined in a moderate character. A soul that spends a lifetime developing the intellect without taking care of the body may later compensate with a lifetime that stresses physical pursuits to the exclusion of the mind. Neither extreme is healthy; but by experiencing each in turn, the soul may collect the necessary experience from which balance of the mental and physical selves may later be achieved.

The key to the law of balance is that it comes into play only when extreme imbalance is exhibited. Also, it will tend to deal with inner qualities of mind or spirit rather than with physical circumstances. It does not, for example, dictate that beauty and ugliness, wealth and poverty, or other such opposite forms of human experience must come in alternating sequence from lifetime to lifetime just because they happen to *be* opposites. The law of balance instead deals with opposite extremes that reflect an immoderate soul. Just as a driver who falls asleep at the wheel when driving along a highway bounded by concrete retainer walls will veer off the barrier on one side and go to the opposite side of the road, the soul that "falls asleep" and loses balance will find itself ricocheting to the opposite extreme. This, too, is a manifestation of how the universe keeps itself in balance.

In considering each of these laws, we can observe karma as a force toward oneness, harmony, and goodness. All of our choices either flow with that force or against it. When they flow with it, the harmony is multiplied; when they flow against it, the resulting discord moves us back in the right direction. In each of the examples we have looked at, choices led to results. As we've already seen, that matter of choice—learning to choose aright—is at the core of our spiritual development through earthly incarnations. Yet some of the stickiest philosophical and practical problems we face in putting the philosophy of reincarnation to work in our lives have to do with clarifying our understanding of choice, what it is, and how we use it. Our next step, then, will be to examine those issues in depth.

7

HOW THE SOUL THINKS AND CHOOSES

Question: *Is the body [individual] aware of the destiny of the physical body at birth?*

Answer: *God Himself knows not what man will destine to do with himself, else would He have repented that He had made man? He has given man free will. Man destines the body!*

EDGAR CAYCE reading no. 262–86

THE CONCEPT OF FREE will is indispensable to the philosophy of reincarnation in the Cayce readings. Without it, the cycles of rebirth would be pointless; for without free will, our experiences in the earth would not be creating a strengthened and mature capacity to choose aright, but would instead be buffeting our souls through a predetermined assortment of sorrows and joys. Where is the growth, where is the learning in such experience? Clearly, the philosophy of reincarnation only makes sense if our experiences are the product of our own choices.

Ironically, it is this cause-and-effect (or karmic) relationship between our choices and our later experiences that leads to one of the greatest popular misconceptions about reincarnation: the idea that in this life we are "destined" to experience certain things "because of our karma."

People new to the idea of reincarnation often believe that karma requires us to be punished for things that "another person" (that is, our own former incarnation) did long ago. So great is the chasm between the current self-concept and the identity of the prior experience, that the influences from one's own past life are regarded as a kind of possession by the spirit of *someone else* who lived in another time. This is probably why we frequently see possession and reincarnation confused in movies. Of course, if we have no grasp of the essential continuity between our current selves and an earlier edition of ourselves in a former lifetime, it is easy to feel predetermined and even victimized by so-called karmic destiny.

Even those who recognize the continuity of the core person (or, to use Edgar Cayce's term, the "entity") from lifetime to lifetime may tend at times to view the events in this life as being somehow predetermined by karmic necessity. For example, many reincarnationists would insist that the soul "chooses" the events of a given lifetime before it ever enters a body and begins a new life. With an understanding of its growth needs, the soul chooses the kind of life that will best help it meet those needs, planning before birth the key events that will be needed. It knows to whom it will be born. It knows the triumphs that lie ahead, and it knows the tragedies as well. It knows the main choices it will face and which choices are consistent with the growth plan. It even knows the span of time it has available to complete the chosen events for the incarnation. In short, the lifetime has been mapped by the soul. If it seems, once the soul's awareness has been swathed in material consciousness, that there is any lack of freedom to choose, it is simply because the conscious person has lost touch with the soul's deeper choices.

Certainly, this latter view places the responsibility for choice more squarely within the individual soul's locus of control than the former one does; still, both views are predeterministic in that they see an extremely limited opportunity for us to face and make choices within the context of the earthly experience. In the first, more drastic predeterministic view, all connection between the current self and the self who caused the current conditions is lost. In the second, more moderate view, total responsibility for the events in one's life is accepted, but the choices are seen as having taken place outside this life and being virtually set in stone once this life is underway. Thus we still have a philosophical struggle between freedom and determinism within the context of any given life. How are we to resolve this conflict?

THE PROBLEM OF CHOICE IN A FIXED WORLD

It is easy to see how such predeterministic views as those described above arise out of the observation of life. Even the most unfettered among us appear to have only limited choice at best. Who is free to have the life partner of his or her choice, simply by choosing it? How many people do we know who are free to take any career of their choosing, regardless of connections or "lucky breaks"? How free *is* the child born in a slum? Or to drug-addicted parents?

To look at it from the other side of the fence, how many of our good "choices" in life have been entirely independent of serendipitous circumstances? Can we really take all of the credit for choosing well when we are among the relative few who find a congenial mate? When our financial choices bring us an abundance of this world's goods, can we *really* say that it was the wisdom of our choices alone that led to success? When learning comes easily, can we truthfully attribute our special expertise in a chosen field to disciplined study alone?

Clearly, the element of what is commonly called chance plays a major part in directing the flow of life's experiences. Yet, if the Cayce readings are correct, there is no such thing as chance. Reincarnation removes both the fortuitous and the unfortunate breaks in life from the domain of chance and places them in the category of effects resulting from causes we ourselves have set in motion. Each circumstance, every person, all conditions that come into our lives have come as part of the purposefulness of that incarnation. So what is the problem? Hasn't the central concept of cause and effect already solved the puzzle of freedom and determinism? Isn't it true that we *are* predetermined by our karma? That within the span of any given lifetime we are meeting an already established destiny? The answer to those questions is yes—and no.

Yes, we are facing the products of our own choices when we encounter seeming chance occurrences in life. But no, we are not predetermined to a series of events nor to opt for certain choices along the way. The problem with any outlook that views our karma as a destiny in life is that such a view is inconsistent with one of the central concepts of reincarnation in the Cayce readings: that making choices in the *earth* is one of the main purposes of *being* in the earth. If we are always living lives that are predetermined by prior lives, or even choices between lives, when and where does the choosing in the flesh come in?

A COMPROMISE BETWEEN FREEDOM AND DESTINY

Some of the philosophical issues related to reincarnation are complicated unnecessarily when we examine them from the perspective of multiple lives. If we think of our life—our soul's life, that is—as *one* life broken into many segments, some of the most confusing issues look considerably more straightforward. This is especially true when it comes to sorting out free will and destiny. If we will step back and look at the way choice works within the context of our *current* life, we will have the key to seeing how it works over the span of many lives.

Choices Build in Complex Chains

Our choices never take place in a vacuum. There is no such thing as "starting from scratch" when it comes to choices, as we are always in the midst of preexisting circumstances when we make a choice. For example, even the simple choice of what you will have for dinner on a given night is made in a context that takes into consideration any number of other factors: what you had for lunch, what you had for dinner the night before, whether you have shopped for groceries recently, whether you want to shop for groceries tonight . . . the list could go on indefinitely. And this is only a choice about what to have for dinner! Imagine the factors that already exist at the time when we choose a mate, when we decide to buy an expensive new car, when we head out on a job interview, or when we select a city or town in which to live. No, there is no such thing as a brand-new choice; all of our choices, however free in the moment, spring out of a context of preexisting factors.

Not only do our choices take place within the context of a variety of preexisting factors, but many of those factors can be readily identified as the results of past choices. In the very simple example of menu choice, we can see that earlier meal choices and choices about shopping led to some of the conditions that will affect the current choice. We could take this principle even further and say that whether your options represented a choice between steak and lobster or a choice between hamburger and tuna casserole might be the result of earlier choices concerning your food budget. Carrying it one step more, the size of your food budget may depend on the salary you collect, which in turn is at least in part the product of earlier choices related to career, study, or the amount of energy you were willing to put into your job. Just so, our earlier choices concerning not only relationships, but also interests, values, lifestyle, and any number of other things will have material impact on the choice of a mate. The same goes for virtually any kind of choice. Choices of every type imaginable will have gone before each "new" choice you make in life. Think of it this way: every choice you make is the most recent link in an ongoing chain of choices.

Losing Sight of Earlier Choices

We feel predestined when we lose sight of our own earlier choices, for it is quite easy to forget that some of our own earlier choices have led us to our present circumstances. The child who bemoans the fact that he must spend all of Sunday evening doing his homework has conveniently forgotten that he chose not to do it earlier. In the same way, we are most inclined to forget our earlier choices when they have led to unpleasant alternatives in the present. Our memories usually function far more effectively when we are choosing in the context of earlier *constructive* choices and we therefore face happy possibilities in our chain of choices!

In all fairness, though, many times we cannot remember our earlier choices because they took place in earlier lives and are therefore truly hidden to conscious awareness. It is then that we are most likely to feel predestined or fated to certain experiences. Yet does the fact that we have forgotten an earlier choice make us any less responsible for it? Does an event become "predestined" simply because we can't remember causing it? More important still, does a *predisposition* due to earlier choices eliminate our freedom to choose in the present? An analogy may help clarify the answers to these questions.

Chains of Choices

We can see that we are in truth free when we trace chains of choices. Suppose a child decides at a very young age that she wants to take piano lessons. Soon after her first lesson, she decides that she wants to be a very good piano player, and so she practices often and long. Over time, her aspiration grows until she knows that what she wants more than anything is to be a professional concert pianist. Because of her goal, many other decisions are shaped accordingly: hours spent in piano practice while some of her classmates are pursuing their own choice to participate in sports; performing in recitals instead of playing on the school softball team; even her circle of friends tends to form around a common interest in music. By the time she becomes an adult, this girl does indeed grow into an accomplished professional musician.

Now suppose at age thirty she says to herself, "I feel the need for a change in my life. I have free will. I have the capacity to shape my life through my choices. I therefore choose to become an Olympic gymnast instead of a concert pianist." And when her attempts to perform Olympic-class gymnastics fail—despite her earnest effort and faithful practice—she says, "Obviously, I was predetermined to be a musician and not an athlete."

We can readily see that it is ludicrous for this woman to attribute her circumstances to fate or destiny. She is obviously experiencing the only logical result of a long series of choices—choices that she freely made. If she is limited, it is only by her own prior choices. And while she may not be free to erase an entire chain of choices by a simple act of will, she *is* free to do one thing: She is free to begin a new direction in her chain of choices. She is free to start developing her athletic skills, even if her past choices away from athletic development make it highly unlikely that she will reach Olympic-level accomplishment after such a late start.

At this point it is natural to ask, what about her past-life experiences? Didn't they make her more inclined to the piano than to athletics in the first place? Of course they did. *But they, in their time, were her own choices just as surely as the choices about lessons and practice were hers in this lifetime.* It is only when we forget that our past-life choices are just as much ours as our current-life choices that we start to think in predeterministic terms. And it is only when we forget that every moment provides us the *free* choice to continue a chain of choices in any direction we choose that we feel "fated" by our own past choices. The secret to reconciling free will with an apparent destiny based on the past is to recognize the influence of our choices on reality itself.

Past Choices Limit Our Freedom

Our freedom is limited to some extent by our past choices. Many of us have at one time or another found ourselves caught in a logical fallacy much like this one: Someone you love is making a long car trip with an expected arrival time no later than 10 P.M. Your loved one has promised you a safe arrival call, which you begin to expect any time after about 9:30. You don't really begin to worry until about 10:30, when the call still hasn't come. At this point you begin to pray, "Dear God, please don't let him/her have been in an accident." Sometimes in such moments our immediate concern drives out any recognition that we are making a totally illogical request of God. Other times an awareness of the reality can't help but slip through: by the time you are praying this prayer, your loved one either has been in an accident or hasn't been. The time to pray that he or she wouldn't be in an accident was when the trip began! To pray that something is or is not the case (as compared with praying that something will or will not happen) is to expect God to alter what is already reality in response to our prayer.

While we may affirm that God has the *ability* to do whatever he chooses, it is also true that God cannot contradict himself. Therefore there are some things that God cannot do—not because he is unable, but because they are logically impossible. For example, it would be a logical impossibility for God to create a square circle. This is not a reflection on God's omnipotence, but on the inherent contradiction in the feat requested. Similarly, literally to undo something that has in fact been done or happened would involve a contradiction of the law of cause and effect—which, as we have already seen, flows from God's very nature. The lawful, harmonious flow of cause and effect in this universe *is* an expression of God, and to suspend that law involves God in the logical impossibility of denying himself. When we expect such things of God, we are thinking *magically;* that is, expecting our wishes to transcend the lawfulness of reality.

What does all of this have to do with our freedom in the face of apparent destiny? When we expect our free will to be able to erase the reality that we have already built through our choices, we are engaging in the same kind of magical thinking that would expect God to change what already is, in answer to our prayers. To some degree, we are stuck with what we currently have to work with—a body that is not as healthy or shapely as we might like; a marriage or romance that involves more rough going than smooth; a child who brings us more heartache than joy; a social life that knows more loneliness or inadequacy than companionship and fulfillment. All of these are conditions that represent the composite of past choices, both in this life and in prior lives. To expect our undesirable situations to change with the snap of our fingers is to expect magic, not freedom.

Yet to be stuck with undesirable circumstances does not mean that it is our karma to endure it patiently as our destiny. A woman once asked me privately during a seminar whether the best way to meet her karma was to put up with her husband's physical abuse. Her question showed that she had taken her understanding of free will far enough to realize that her current situation was the product of her own past choices. But she hadn't taken it quite far enough to see that her free will now presented her with the opportunity to make the most constructive choices possible concerning this destructive relationship. Her acknowledgment of free will had yet to remove her from the role of victim. She had merely moved from being victimized by her husband to being victimized by her own past choices. True freedom, creative use of free will, always leaves us free to choose *in any moment* the direction in which our chain of choices will now lead.

"THINKING" ON THE SOUL LEVEL

Another confusing aspect of free will and soul-level choices has to do with our concept of how the soul thinks and chooses. Especially when we talk of hard-

ships, handicaps, and adversities as not being imposed
from outside of ourselves, but rather as taken on by the
soul, it can stretch our credulity to think that such conditions really are voluntary. People will often ask me in
seminars, "Do you mean to say that some people have
actually *chosen* to come into this life without their eye-
sight or without a limb or knowing they are going to
starve to death in Africa? I just can't imagine anyone
choosing such things." The stock answer to such questions is that our souls have our higher good in mind, and
are therefore willing to endure temporal suffering for
the sake of the lessons learned or the spiritual growth it
brings.

The problem with this kind of answer, however, is
that it seems to fragment our notion of the self, conjur-
ing up overly simplistic images of a thinking, choosing
soul separate from the only self (the conscious self) with
which we tend to identify. Just as the woman in the
example cited above substituted victimization by her
own choices for victimization by her husband, this popular image of a choosing "higher Self" subjecting us to
adversity merely substitutes a moralizing, judging soul
for a retributive, judging God. It is easy enough for the
higher Self to say, "I think it will be necessary to be
deserted by my wife in the next lifetime in order to learn
that I shouldn't have deserted mine last time"; the
higher Self won't be the one who does the suffering
when the desertion occurs! It will be the poor, bewildered lower self who takes the brunt of what the higher
Self chose to take on.

An alternative understanding of how the soul voluntarily takes on hardship arises from our earlier consideration of how the law of karma works. A soul that "wakes
up" to its disharmony with the ultimate harmony of the
universe is a soul that "chooses" to experience the resulting consequence as a means of regaining spiritual
equilibrium. But that "choosing" seems to be substan-

tially different from the choosing that goes on in our conscious minds day by day. When we choose a career or a spouse or a vacation, for example, there are two very important elements: the reflective, choosing self and the person, thing, or activity chosen. We experience ourselves as separate from the object of our choices. As a separate, choosing consciousness, we bring our own desires, motivations, fears, and even biases and blind spots to bear on each decision in our lives.

By contrast, the choosing we do on a soul level has more to do with *forces* at work than with reflective decision making. At the level of consciousness where soul-level choices are made, there is not so much a perfectly motivated higher Self choosing "what's best" even when it hurts, but rather an *awareness* that necessarily sets certain forces in motion. That awareness involves the soul's recognition of the Oneness of which it is a portion. With that recognition of Oneness comes a corresponding awareness that knows which experiences are in harmony with Oneness and which are not. That realization in turn acts like a magnetic force that draws certain life experiences to the soul in the next incarnation. All of the experiences, both pleasant and unpleasant, are the product of past choices, and all have in a sense been chosen by the soul. But they have not been chosen in the sense of a disconnected higher Self bestowing or imposing an experience on the conscious person who must make the best of his or her assignment. The choosing happens when we create *conditions* that set forces in motion which draw certain experiences to us.

CHOOSING YOUR PARENTS AND YOUR PHYSICAL BODY

The complexity of choice on the soul level is nowhere more apparent than in the "choice" of a physical body and the parents to whom one is born. Here, too, there may be a tendency to oversimplify the issue. When we think of a soul choosing a body and parents, it is all too easy to conjure up images of souls floating around in a disembodied state between lifetimes, and periodically choosing to incarnate the way we might choose a house to buy or a wardrobe to wear. We can imagine this disembodied soul "deciding" that it is time to come back to earth for another round of lessons, and subsequently looking over the entrance opportunities available—surveying the pregnant women and the family relationship potentials involved with each and ultimately saying, "I'll take that one!" Such notions are not only too simplistic to accommodate a deeper understanding of how reincarnation works, they also create embarrassing contradictions with what we know from science about the major determinants of human characteristics.

Does reincarnation, with its stress on past-life influences as determinants of who we are, deny what modern biology can tell us about the vital role of genes in creating our makeup? When we point to past experiences as the sources of fears and talents and strengths and weaknesses, must we ignore what psychology and social science tell us about the impact our upbringing and our environment have on each one of us? How *can* we reconcile past-life influences and the idea that a soul chooses a body with what the best of biological and social science have to tell us?

The answer to this apparent contradiction lies somewhere between the position that would make heredity and environment the sole shapers of our destiny, and the opposite view that would deny their power completely. The middle ground allows for an interaction between past-life influences and the present-life influences we call heredity and environment. Hereditary and environmental influences are indeed very real causes in our lives. But they are not *first* causes; that is, causes were set in motion *before* we each inherited a body, parents, and a set of childhood experiences. Those causes were the choices and experiences of prior lives, and it was that set of past-life causes that determined which genetic background—out of the billions of possibilities— our soul was drawn into. Similarly, those same past-life causes determine which environmental conditions we are drawn into in a new incarnation.

In the light of what we have already seen about the way choices work in chains, very little active choosing is going on by the time a soul is being drawn into a body. Instead, the soul is drawn with something like magnetic attraction to just the right genetic heritage and family background to reflect that soul's history and current growth needs. The nonphysical part of each one of us, as the composite record of all of our choices and experiences, seems actually to be "shaped" to reflect the choices we have made. The abilities developed over various lifetimes have left their mark. The wounds, both physical and emotional, that we have dwelled on have left their scars. The love we have nurtured, the goals we have aspired to, virtually every imaginable facet of earthly experience has left its mark, "shaping" the nonphysical self. At every moment, our nonphysical "shape" is the composite of all of our experiences up until that time. And it is this "shape," rather than reflective choosing, that selects the body, family, environment, and other circumstances we are born into.

At the moment of entry into a new physical form, the uniquely shaped nonphysical self is drawn to the body that fits it, and to the family environment that best reflects its history and needs. Thus heredity and environment are real forces at work, even in a reincarnationist framework. We *can* link physical traits, creativity, intelligence, and other characteristics to the genetic heritage we have received. We *can* trace a cause-and-effect relationship between aspects of the childhood environment and later aspects of character and personality. But, in the reincarnationist worldview, that childhood environment and genetic heritage are not a hand randomly dealt as we entered this life; rather, it is the natural, logical reflection of what we have brought in with us on a soul level.

Part III

USING PAST-LIFE MEMORY

In the studies, then, know where you are going. To find that ye only lived, died and were buried under the cherry tree in Grandmother's garden does not make thee one whit better neighbor, citizen, mother or father! But to know that ye spoke unkindly and suffered for it, and in the present may correct it by being righteous—that is worthwhile!
EDGAR CAYCE reading no. 5753–2

8

PAST-LIFE MEMORY AND SOUL GROWTH

In man's analysis and understanding of himself, it is [as] well to know from whence he came as to know whither he is going.

EDGAR CAYCE reading no. 5753–1

MOST PEOPLE WHO SERIOUSLY consider reincarnation as a personal philosophy begin to wonder sooner or later about their own past lives. When and where have I lived? Who and what was I? Who among my current loved ones was also in my life in the past? Are my difficult relationships continuations of old conflicts from past lives? Where did my current-life problems start? Where did my special interests or talents come from? On and on the questions go; and underlying all of them is often the nagging doubt, "If there is such a thing as reincarnation, why can't I remember my past lives?" Or, from the more optimistic seeker, "Where can I find someone who will tell me about/help me remember my past lives?"

Although some may be quick to dismiss these questions as idle curiosity, such thoughts actually reflect our natural desire to know ourselves more fully. What thought could be more tantalizing to the inquisitive mind than that we have had personal experiences in exotic settings and distant historical periods? What could be more natural than the desire to claim these lost

memories, thus expanding our sense of who we really
are? In fact, what could be more instructive to our personal growth than the addition of hundreds and even
thousands of lifetimes into our experience bank? Idle
curiosity? We may as well call the entire field of scientific inquiry "idle curiosity"; for isn't curiosity the beginning of most knowledge?

The Cayce reading that I chose to head this chapter
underscores just how valuable past-life knowledge may
be, when it suggests that it is just as important to know
where we have been as it is to know where we are going.
When we stop to consider how very important it is to
know where we are going, the full impact of this statement hits us. After all, virtually any formula for success
in life will tell you that knowing where you are going—
identifying your goals and making realistic plans to
reach them—is central to achievement. Whether you're
trying to lose weight, learn a new job skill, become more
socially adept, be a better time manager, or whatever
your chosen area of self-improvement may be, you can
be sure that learning to recognize where you're headed
will be a significant part of what the experts have to
teach you. And here we have the Cayce readings suggesting that it is every bit as important to know about
where you have already been.

The past-life significance of such a statement is unavoidable. Clearly, there is a tremendous growth potential in knowledge of our past, presumably because that
knowledge will better equip us to respond to present
conditions with the greater wisdom that experience
brings. This concept is reminiscent of the statement by
philosopher George Santayana: "Those who cannot remember the past are condemned to repeat it." It is natural, then, for those who have accepted the personal
responsibility that reincarnation implies to chafe at the
limitations of normal consciousness, to want to know
more about their own past, and even to feel a certain

indignation at the lack of memory that most of us seem to bring into each new lifetime. How *is* the reincarnationist to deal with the fact that past-life memory seems to be the exception rather than the rule in life?

THE PARADOX OF MEMORY AND FORGETFULNESS

If knowledge of the past can be so conducive to growth, why have most of us forgotten the majority of our past lives? There are four main reasons that forgetfulness is a natural part of our soul progression from lifetime to lifetime, as we will now consider: it comes naturally with the passage of time; it allows us to start each life afresh; it can guard against complacency; and it lets us grow at a pace we can handle.

Forgetfulness Comes Naturally with the Passage of Time

On the most practical level, we can explain the absence of past-life memory the same way we explain the absence of memory from very early periods in the current life. How many of us can clearly remember events from our preschool years? Some people have memories that go this far back, but many do not. How many can remember their first birthday? Or learning to walk? Or being born? Few people indeed can remember such early events in their normal, conscious frame of mind. Yet we would not conclude that these events did not occur or that they were developmentally insignificant because the person who experienced them carries no conscious recollection of the experience.

If we have forgotten key events that are so recent as to have occurred within this life, why would we expect to remember even further back, to lives that took place hundreds or even thousands of years ago? Just as we can acknowledge the psychological impact of experiences long-since forgotten within the framework of this current life, we can see that past-life experiences, though consciously forgotten, can still play a major role in shaping us into the people we are today, psychologically and spiritually.

Still, this may appear to be begging the question. For if it is true that this process of incarnating in the earth has been provided by a loving Creator as the best means for us to come into our full maturity as souls, couldn't that Creator have made us with better memories? We often feel an understandable sense of injustice in the idea that we should be put here to learn from our experiences, and yet have such woefully inadequate memories come as standard equipment for the assignment. For the range of experience that the soul must accumulate over the course of its earthly sojourns, one would think that a far more acute capacity to recall would have been provided. Yet perhaps it is in the forgetfulness even more than in the memory that we can find the greatest evidence of the careful plan behind our opportunities in earthly consciousness.

Forgetfulness Gives Us a Fresh Start Each Lifetime

Our eagerness to know more, and the potential helpfulness of such knowledge notwithstanding, we don't have to look very far in the Cayce readings to see that *full* knowledge of the past is not necessarily a good thing. If this material is correct, we've probably all been heroes and we've probably all been villains at various times in our soul history; and conscious awareness of some of the peaks and valleys of our soul history must come only

selectively, when we are in the best position to understand and make constructive use of that knowledge.

Consider, for example, the reading in which Cayce
was asked about the soul we know of as Judas Iscariot.
Cayce did link that identity with someone living at that
time, but went on to say that this soul was living a constructive life, with no inkling of the part he had played
in that all-important drama of long ago. It is clear from
Cayce's treatment of this question that knowledge of his
life as Judas was not of prime importance to this individual at that time. Rather, he recommended that this
person be exposed to spiritual work in a more general
way. It is easy to imagine why that soul was not yet
ready to face the memory of his experience as Judas,
and it is equally clear from Cayce's response that such
blindness to his past did not indicate lack of progress.

How many of us carry memories that would have an
equally devastating effect on our growth? We may not
have played the roles of famed malefactors, but what
about the dormant memories of spouses and children
we may have hurt in some way? Friends we may have
betrayed? People we may have killed or maimed? One
young woman reports the chilling effect of an unsolic-
ited psychic revelation that told her she had sacrificed
children to a fire god in an ancient culture. Regardless
of whether the psychic who volunteered this information was accurate, the woman was not prepared to handle this alleged experience constructively; at the time
she could only alternate between denial that it was true
and tremendous guilt at the thought that it might be
true.

Experiences in which we were the victims rather than
the perpetrators can be equally debilitating if we learn
of them at inopportune times. Just as guilt and self-
condemnation can result from premature knowledge of
our mistakes, so can emotional pain, fear, and condem-

nation of others arise from untimely awareness of past suffering.

When we consider the mental and spiritual anguish that might accompany memory of some of our less pleasant past experiences, it is easy to see that the veil of forgetfulness that slips over our consciousness at birth is a blessing rather than a curse. For in each new incarnation, we are shielded from the memories that would be more than we could consciously handle. In a very real sense, we start each life with a clean slate, so far as conscious awareness is concerned; while on the unconscious level every memory—in fact, *all* of the cumulative experience that is germane to that life's lessons —is there for us to draw upon.

Forgetfulness Can Guard Us Against Complacency

Not only is it sometimes best for us to forget past traumas, but even our greatest accomplishments may best be left in the unconscious memory at times. A stereotype of the nutty reincarnationist is the man who thinks he was Napoleon and the woman who thinks she was Cleopatra in a past life. We may bristle at such a shallow portrayal of people who embrace a philosophy that can in truth be inexpressibly profound, but it may be worthwhile for us to search for the kernel of truth behind the exaggeration of stereotype. If we look honestly and deeply enough, we probably will see that many of us are at times tempted to grasp for visions of past accomplishments as justification for a mediocre present, or as an excuse not to work on personal shortcomings. For example, the reincarnationist who says, "I know that the reason my coworkers resent me is because I used to be very rich and important and they were my servants" is probably hiding from some personal traits that should be acknowledged and worked on. Similarly, the person who says, "In my last life, I was a very powerful leader who carried a great load of responsibility, and this life is my chance to relax," is most likely using reincarnation as an excuse for laziness. In short, if knowledge of past accomplishments would tend to make you coast through life now, contentedly resting on your laurels, then you are better off blissfully unaware of your glorious achievements in the past.

Forgetfulness Allows Us to Face Our Growth Areas at a Pace We Can Handle

Stop and think for a moment just what it means to be an eternal soul. Try to fathom the number of times you have walked this earth, collecting loved ones as well as hated enemies, facing experiences that awakened every emotion known to the human psyche, meeting trials and tests, receiving blessings and opportunities to grow in wisdom and love and spiritual awareness. It is nothing short of mind-boggling to contemplate both the quantity and variety of life experiences any given soul carries somewhere in the depths of memory. Can you imagine carrying all of these in consciousness? If you have ever tossed and turned on a sleepless night, thinking of all of the things you needed to get done at home, at work, or in preparation for a holiday or other major event, you will appreciate how overwhelming it would be to carry full consciousness of all of our lives and the growth experiences those lives entail.

The sheer volume of soul-development lessons each one of us must master is so great that the only practical way to approach the task is to break it down into "life-sized" portions; that is, our time-bound, limited-memory experience in the earth breaks what is ultimately an eternity's worth of growth into discreet experiences that we can learn from, one at a time. If we could remember all of our past lives, the ability of time to sort out and organize our growth experiences would be lost. We would instead face the overwhelming awareness of our total growth agendas all at once, and very likely end up in a paralysis of inaction, not knowing where to begin.

On many occasions, Edgar Cayce identified the three dimensions of this world as time, space, and patience. A rather peculiar grouping of concepts, and one that has puzzled many a student of the readings. Where does patience fit in with the other two dimensions? From the standpoint of the soul's eternal nature and its history in the time- and space-bound plane of the earth, we may see the role of patience in a new light. For it is the apportioning role of time and space, breaking our eternal experience down into "life-sized" portions, that creates *patience,* or the capacity to accomplish our soul agendas systematically, one step at a time.

For all of the reasons given above, we can see why wholesale memory of our past lives would not be particularly helpful. We are not always ready to face the traumas of our past. We are not always spiritually mature enough to take our accomplishments in stride. Nor are we capable of facing the totality of the growth issues that our complete experience in the earth represents. At those times, it is best for learning to take place on the unconscious level; for it is totally possible to grow and learn without direct, conscious awareness of the past. Just as one can feed data into a computer, understand a new arrangement of that data when it appears on the screen, and yet never understand the processing of the data that went on within the computer's circuitry, we can feed experience into the subconscious levels of awareness where it is correlated with past-life experiences, and the learning that takes place eventually changes us on an outer level as well.

Still, as we have already considered, there *is* a place

for past-life memory in the path of soul development. In fact, as we shall see, past-life memory is as much a part of the lesson plan as forgetfulness is.

SELECTIVE PAST-LIFE MEMORY IS A PART OF DAILY LIFE

To some degree, it is misleading to imply that past-life experiences are locked away in the depths of the unconscious mind, and that we can choose either to awaken them or to leave them sleeping. We do have some control over our relative level of conscious awareness of past-life experiences, and we will explore the avenues of past-life memory stimulation in some depth in chapters nine and ten. But it is equally true that past-life memory is an ongoing part of our psychological and spiritual makeup; and to think that we can choose to leave memories of former experiences completely out of our lives is to assume a power of disassociation that is beyond our capability. Some reincarnationists who are not inclined to explore past lives will say, "I have enough to worry about in this life without dredging up past-life memories as well." This may sound like a very commonsense approach, but the choice to remember may not be so completely within our power as such a stance assumes.

Just as we cannot disconnect ourselves from the early childhood memories that have impact on making us the adult people we are today, we cannot disconnect ourselves entirely from our past-life memories. It may be tempting at times to think that we can keep our lives more simple by focusing entirely on the here and now, leaving past-life concerns out of the picture; but the evidence in the Cayce life readings suggests that past-life memories influence us continually, whether we recognize them or not. As we shall see shortly, our personalities, our interests and abilities, our fears, our childhood experiences, and even our bodies are unconscious expressions of past-life memories.

Our choice, then, is not so much whether to remember or not remember, but whether to learn to recognize, direct, and channel those memories to our benefit. This intriguing and enlightening process of personal past-life exploration will be the primary focus of the next two chapters; but before we delve into that topic specifically, let's clarify the reasons why selective knowledge of past lives can be helpful.

THE VALUE OF SELECTIVELY ENHANCED PAST-LIFE MEMORY

We have now looked at the value of both memory and forgetfulness in the soul's journey from lifetime to lifetime. We have seen that the benefit of memory from our cumulative experience can make us wiser, but that too much memory of our soul's experience can sidetrack us or overwhelm us. How do we walk that thin line between helpful and counterproductive memory? When we explore our past, can we know which kind of memory we'll be getting? These questions frequently arise for the conscientious past-life explorer. Side by side with eagerness to know more comes the uneasy concern that we may end up learning more than is good for us.

In answer to this question, the first thing to keep in mind about potentially damaging memories is that their potential to damage is precisely the reason that forgetfulness has been *built into* the nature of human consciousness. The types of memory that would retard growth or be too much to handle were mentioned above as examples of why we *can't* remember all of our lives. By contrast, the influence of memories that are relevant to our current lives was mentioned as an example of how *helpful* memories are relatively close to conscious awareness. In other words, those memories that would not be helpful are exactly the ones that are not about to come seeping through into conscious awareness and take us by surprise. It may sound like a tautology, but those memories that we *can* become aware of are the ones that hold the potential to help us do a better job with the challenges and opportunities we face in the here and now. To the extent that we are ready to grapple with personal and soul growth in this life, we can benefit from the added insights of increased past-life awareness in the following ways.

Freedom from Limitations

Past-life insight helps free us from the limitations of unconscious motivations. One of the rudiments of biofeedback training is to teach the student how to recognize the ways that he or she unconsciously perpetuates the very physical habits that increase stress, elevate blood pressure, or exacerbate pain. The feedback system signals the student each time he or she unconsciously does those things that bring undesirable physical results. Eventually, the awareness of a previously unconscious act turns into the power to consciously control something that was originally beyond conscious direction. At that point, the biofeedback has taught the individual how to stop an unwanted, unconscious pattern of response.

The same principle works with undesirable past-life carryovers. As the Tibetan Buddhist thinker Lama Govinda expresses it in *Creative Meditation,* the "undissolved and undigested" past experiences that "sink into the subconscious" become "the germ of uncontrollable —because unconscious—drives and impulses." We can see a close parallel to the biofeedback process when Govinda goes on to prescribe enhanced past-life awareness as the key to release us from these drives and impulses. Govinda says that by becoming conscious of his past, the Buddha "freed himself from the power of hidden causes."

Freeing ourselves from the power of hidden causes is, to a large extent, what serious past-life work is all about. Discovering that you are reacting automatically to experiences in this life because of past-life experiences that have left you feeling threatened, betrayed, or angry can be a major breakthrough in overcoming unwelcome emotional patterns.

For example, a woman realized that a past-life experience of abandonment had made her extremely sensitive to any perceived threat of abandonment in this life. Because of this, she was better able to separate past experiences from present reality and establish a more secure outlook this time around. A young man was not aware that his intense pursuit of spiritual growth was turning him into a recluse until he learned of several past lives as a monk. This knowledge helped him recognize a previously unconscious tendency to pair spirituality with separation from the world. With that understanding, he was better equipped to decide consciously whether monk-like seclusion was part of his chosen path in his current lifetime, or whether he preferred to blend his spiritual quest with a more secular life.

These are but two examples of people who might have failed to choose their perspectives, reactions, and directions in life, simply because they were on automatic pilot, motivated by unconscious associations and experiences from the past. As we can see in these cases, selective knowledge of those lives that are unconsciously motivating us can emancipate us from unwanted influences and enable us to choose anew.

Meeting Life's Difficulties Constructively

Past-life insight can empower us to meet life's difficulties constructively. When we can claim this benefit of
past-life insight, we have transformed philosophical con-
victions about reincarnation into personal, practical understandings that help us meet life's challenges. At the
most *impersonal* level, reincarnation is merely a philo-
sophically comforting belief. It makes sense out of the
seeming inequities in life and puts suffering and hardship in a larger perspective that at least removes the
cosmic cruelty such adversity implies, if not the suffering and hardship itself. That is, the philosophy of reincarnation does not make human suffering any less real,
but it can ameliorate it in the sense that it incorporates
it into a larger purpose. However, it is when we are able
to apply the philosophical framework to real-life situations that the transformative power of the philosophy is
released. Nowhere is this more true than in coping with
life's challenges and adversities; and nowhere does the
vital importance of knowing one's *own* past become
more apparent.

Suppose, for example, that you find yourself in the
role of a victim. Perhaps someone has sabotaged an important personal relationship, or betrayed your trust.
You may even have been robbed or physically harmed.
Maybe a series of bad breaks has hurt you financially or
in your career advancement. These are just a few of the
countless situations in which it is natural to feel victimized by another's actions or by circumstances. Hurt, resentment, fear, or desire for revenge are among some of
the most likely responses to such experiences. But, understandable though those responses may be, they are
also harmful to you. They worsen an already bad situation, leading you into destructive emotions at best or
destructive actions at worst. At such times, the mere

desire to control negative responses can be unequal to
the task. You may believe on a philosophical level that
everything happens for a purpose, but it can be difficult
to respond and act from that perspective when the challenge comes.

Yet suppose that you *did* understand, from a past-life
perspective, why this "bad" thing had happened to you.
Suppose you had insight concerning the prior choices
and experiences that have brought this current circumstance into your life. That insight can make the difference between being a victim of or a victor over life's
hardships.

Awakening Latent Talents

Past-life insight awakens latent talents and abilities. Not
only does an understanding of past experiences help us
meet life's challenges and free us from limiting emotions and behavior patterns, but it can also open the
door to undreamed potentials. The vast soul history we
each bring into this life includes the accomplishments
we've been accumulating since the dawn of earthly experience. Lives in which we have mastered the ability to
paint pictures, lead nations, build cities, understand the
mysteries of the cosmos, heal the sick, or counsel the
troubled are just the merest sampling of the kind of
experience that repose in the soul memory of each one
of us.

Not every soul has mastered every talent imaginable,
but it is probably safe to say that we have all mastered
far more, at one time or another, than we would ever
imagine. Just as the difficult past experiences that are
relevant to this life's growth issues are the ones most
accessible to us, the lives in which we learned the special
skills that will most help us now are the ones closest to
conscious awakening. Consider the example of a mid-

dle-aged woman who had always wanted to oil paint. Drawn as she was to this form of creative expression, she just could not believe that she had the talent for it. She reasoned that if it had been there, the ability to paint would have surfaced earlier in life. Consequently, she made only tentative, sporadic attempts at painting that always left her dissatisfied with the result. It was not until she learned of a past life as a reasonably successful painter that she found the self-confidence to take up painting in earnest. To her surprise and delight, she discovered a definite talent and a whole new aspect of herself in the process.

Of course, in this example, the ability to paint was in the woman's makeup, and she could have drawn on it even without the past-life understanding. But like so many of us, she let a lack of belief in herself stand in the way. Getting in touch with a life in which she had successfully met the artistic challenge made a world of difference to her self-image, freeing up the latent talent within her. We each have those potentials in our lives that call to us and urge us to explore new areas of expression and expertise. But far too often, like the woman in our example, we call these urges pipe dreams and tell ourselves that while other people can play a concerto or run for city council or manage a successful business, we could not possibly attain such things. At those times we may find that a past-life insight gives us just the boost we need to transform pipe dreams into reality.

Just how do we get those past-life insights? The answer to this question will be the focus of the next two chapters.

9

PATHWAYS TO PAST-LIFE KNOWLEDGE

*One may ask, as this entity, "Why, then, does one
not recall more often those experiences?"*

*The same may be asked of why there is not the
remembering of the time when two and two to the
entity became four, or when C-A-T spelled cat. It
always did! Ye only became aware of same as it
became necessary for its practical application in the
experience!*

*So with the application of self's experience in
material sojourns. When the necessity arises, as to
how, where and in what direction those
opportunities were applied, the entity brings those
influences to bear in its relationships to daily
problems.*

EDGAR CAYCE reading no. 2301–4

NATURAL CURIOSITY IS USUALLY more than
enough to make us want to know about our past lives.
When we add to that curiosity the realization that very
real growth experiences can come with enhanced past-
life knowledge, the motivation is multiplied. As we have
seen, *selective* enhancement of past-life memories is a
healthy part of personal and spiritual growth. But what
are the various options open to the past-life seeker? Is it
really possible to know our past lives? Can we learn to

make our unconscious memories more accessible to the conscious mind?

SOURCES OF PAST-LIFE KNOWLEDGE

The Cayce readings offer evidence of at least three major categories of past-life information: psychic readings, the unconscious mind, and everyday life experiences. All have the potential to open new levels of understanding about ourselves, and all have their limitations. If we can learn to recognize both the advantages and the responsibilities that come to us when we use each of these sources, we are in the best position to evaluate and use *all* of the resources available to us.

Psychic Readings

The possibility that we can learn about our past lives through psychic readings is especially appealing for many people. There is an immediacy to this source of past-life knowledge, in the sense that we will usually be given fairly coherent accounts of one or more complete lifetimes within the span of one reading. We do not have to wait for memories to emerge, or go through the painstaking process of putting fragments of memory together in order to construct a whole scenario. Perhaps best of all, there is the sense of objectivity that comes with insights offered by a stranger (or at least someone other than oneself)—and a stranger who professes to have psychic perception at that.

For all of these reasons, it is understandable that past-life readings are often the first avenue people think of when they are ready to explore their past lives. It was the approach used by the hundreds of people who came to Edgar Cayce for life readings, and we can all be glad they did take this approach. For, without their requests for these readings, we would not today have the benefit of the body of information that emerged in response to those requests. In the contemporary setting, there is a real place for continued experimentation with psychic sources and the special insights they can offer for our consideration and evaluation.

Nonetheless we should be aware of the limitations and the special responsibilities that come to all of us who seek past-life information through those sources. A psychic past-life reading holds a kind of dazzling allure for many seekers because it seems to promise a level of validity that is not available to us in any other way. In seminars, when I have given examples of past-life insights gained through the personal methods discussed below, participants often ask, "Have you (or the person in question) had this verified with a psychic reading?" I believe the assumptions underlying such a question need to be challenged if we are to engage in healthy, responsible past-life exploration. For it is when we assume that *any* source can provide us with definitive truth, independent of our evaluation, that we run the risk of grave deception, abdication of our personal responsibility to choose for ourselves, or both.

There is no such thing as a completely accurate psychic. Edgar Cayce was not infallible, and neither is any contemporary psychic. Some psychics have better track records than others. This leads many seekers to think that if they can just find a psychic with a good accuracy record, one who comes highly recommended by people whose judgment they trust, *then* it is okay to approach that psychic with the general assumption that what he or she says will be accurate. The problem with this approach is that even good psychics have good days and bad days, or good connections with some clients and fuzzy connections with others. More confusing still, even a good psychic on a good day with a good connection will most likely give a reading that contains *some* distortion or inaccuracy amidst an otherwise reliable account.

This is why Edgar Cayce urged people to test the accuracy of the things he said in his readings, and why he discouraged people from taking his readings on authority, assuming they were true simply because he said them. Not only is it important that we evaluate all psychic information in order to sort out truth from nontruth, but even more important is the personal involvement that comes with such a sorting process.

For example, say you receive a psychic reading that tells you that you were the son of a priest in ancient Egypt, and that you rebelled against the religious order of the day and suffered for it. Something very important to your growth can happen when you take the time to evaluate that information. First, you "try it on for size," measuring the inner traits and tendencies that such a past life would imply against your very best self-knowledge. Then you reconsider key events of your life thus far against the backdrop implied by the reading and see if there are any parallels. You focus on major decisions, challenges, and opportunities in your life at the moment and consider whether the rebellious-son-of-an-Egyptian-priest scenario is meaningful in the context of these current issues.

As you do these things, you will get a better sense of how likely it is that the reading is on target; but far more valuable is the exercise in self-knowledge that has gone into the process. This careful comparison of your current self, life, and key decisions against the lives "revealed" in a psychic reading is at the heart of responsible past-life exploration. It is an example of the use of psychic readings at their best.

Your Own Unconscious Mind

If psychic readings leave us with the major task of relating the information to our personal makeup and life issues, past-life information from our own unconscious mind seems the perfect alternative. What could be more relevant than information that flows from within our own psyche? Not only is information from the unconscious mind personally relevant, it is also a step or two removed from the presumptions and biases of normal, waking consciousness. If the unconscious mind is the repository of past-life memory, what better place to go for knowledge of former incarnations?

For all of these reasons, the hypnotic regression—in which the seeker is taken further and further back in memory until he or she reaches an earlier lifetime— rivals the psychic reading as the preferred approach among many past-life seekers. Less well-known are some of the nonhypnotic avenues to unconscious memory, such as guided (or self-guided) reveries, dreams, "flashes" during meditation, or even waking visions. Proficiency in the use of these latter approaches can be cultivated by anyone interested in pursuing his or her past, where regressions are typically conducted by someone familiar with hypnotic induction. But whatever the specific approach, all past-life insight from the unconscious mind, whether gathered under the guidance of a hypnotist or collected through self-taught techniques, is subject to its own set of limitations that must be taken side-by-side with its potentials.

Just as it is a mistake to assume 100 percent accuracy for a psychic reading, it is equally misleading to assume that one's own unconscious mind is capable of delivering up to us the "truth, the whole truth, and nothing but the truth." A sorting and weighing process similar to the one described with respect to a psychic reading must be applied to past lives that we ourselves may describe in a regression, or see in a dream, reverie, or vision. There is no guarantee that imagination, motivated distortion, or simple misinformation will not creep into the unconscious and color our memories. In fact, one of the most frequent disappointments of people being regressed for the first time is the sense that they have been making up everything they say about their supposed past lives.

There is a common misconception that a *real* regression is an experience in which you go out cold, talk of times and places you've never thought of before, and have no knowledge of what has transpired until some-one plays a tape or reads a transcript of the session. Understandably, this image has led to the widespread belief that a hypnotic regression is the only sure way to get in touch with "genuine" past-life memories. Other approaches pale by comparison to the popular image of a hypnotic regression.

Unfortunately, this image is far from accurate. Although it is true that some of the more dramatic cases involve such complete abandonment of consciousness and total departure from conscious interests and knowledge, the great majority of regressions are far more like normal consciousness than we might expect them to be. There is usually no loss of conscious awareness, though the subject will often experience a very relaxed dreaminess and a distortion of normal time sense. You hear sounds going on in the room, but they don't seem to matter very much in the detached frame of mind that a regression involves. In response to the suggestions and questions of the conductor, most subjects will experience something like a dual consciousness—one part of the mind comes up with images and answers, while the other part of the mind monitors and censors those images and answers with thoughts like, "I'm just making this up," "Now why did I say *that*? What I *should* have said was . . . ," or "How do I answer that question?" If we're not careful, this little monitor within can spoil the experience. It will tell us that we are not really "under," that "it's not working," or that we are just weaving a tall tale.

All of these reactions of disappointment spring from the misconception that, under the right conditions, the unconscious mind will serve up totally reliable past-life information that we can take as objective truth. When the obvious intrusions of conscious awareness enter into the regression experience, we tend to disqualify the particular regression, rather than rethink the original expectations. In fact, all we can know with any degree of surety about the contents of a regression is that they are the significant product of the subject's own unconscious mind and are therefore well worth careful scrutiny. Like the psychic reading, the hypnotic regression invites us to discover our own truth through an intense evaluation process. Because it does spring from within, the relevancy factor is likely to be much more apparent than it might be for information given by someone other than ourselves.

Insights from the unconscious mind that are not hypnotically induced take on greater relative credibility when we realize that hypnosis does not guarantee freedom from imagination, error, or distortion. Dreams, for example, are a rich source of past-life information that flows past our awareness on an almost-nightly basis. (In the next chapter, we will examine some specific ways to use dreams to aid past-life recall.) The regular practice of meditation not only facilitates movement in consciousness to the deeper levels of awareness where past-life memories reside, but it also helps us get in touch with the spiritual growth needs that will put the best motivation behind past-life exploration. Reveries can be a pleasant and nonthreatening way to become comfortable with imagination as a lead-in to the flow of unconscious memory into the thoughts and images of consciousness. Like the hypnotic regression, each of these approaches provides psychologically significant raw material from which we can derive a greater understanding of our past lives.

Everyday Life Experiences

Perhaps the most abundant flow of past-life experiences comes from everyday life itself. Certainly it is the least dramatic and exotic approach to past-life exploration, but the careful observation of our likes and dislikes, habits and inclinations, reactions to things we see and hear and read about, our fears, our hobbies, and our interests can be one of the most fruitful avenues of past-life research. We will deal with this approach more specifically in the following chapter, so we will defer the question of how to go about gleaning past-life knowledge from everyday life until then. For now, let's examine both the special advantages and the drawbacks to this approach.

If the real work of past-life exploration is to use knowledge of the past to do a better job with the present, then surely the everyday experiences and reactions of the present will offer only the most germane past-life insights. If the seeds of your struggle over a career change, for example, lie in a past life, then it is within your current struggle that you can be sure to find the most important clues to the past. That knowledge of the past will in turn help you to make a more enlightened decision concerning the career change. If a difficult personal relationship began in a prior incarnation, then it is within the dynamics of the present difficult relationship that you can expect to find significant traces of the past life in question. Insights developed concerning that past life will shed additional light on current difficulties.

Thus a helpful reciprocal relationship exists between insights related to past and present conditions.

Learning to recognize the clues that bring these past-life insights can take time, but the resultant expansion of understanding is usually well worth the effort. Also, because the approach that gleans clues from everyday life deals with those things that are already part of conscious awareness to some degree, it is usually less emotionally charged than approaches that invite direct input from the unconscious mind. This is not to say that dreams, reveries, meditation insights, or even regressions under the guidance of a capable conductor are going to catapult the seeker into emotionally devastating experiences; unless there is already an emotional imbalance, the unconscious mind is not inclined in most cases to release memory beyond the seeker's ability to cope. But anyone who is uneasy about encountering difficult or painful memories might choose to work consciously with everyday-life clues as the least intrusive of all approaches to past-life exploration.

Admittedly this is the slowest, most gradual road to past-life knowledge, as we will see in the next chapter. It also requires the seeker to figure things out. Because you have no coherent past-life scenario to start with, you must build one from the information at hand. That might seem far less efficient than getting a "ready-made" scenario from a reading or regression. But in fact, it is in the process of *constructing* a past-life understanding from the clues offered in everyday life that real growth happens. For it is during this process that we must scrutinize not only what we do, but also when and why we do it, and with what results.

PRINCIPLES THAT APPLY TO ALL PAST-LIFE INFORMATION

By now some readers may be thoroughly frustrated. For it turns out that none of the major sources of past-life information offers the kind of validity that lets us know for sure that we have really uncovered a genuine past life that actually happened at some other time in history. We have seen that no matter what the source, we must subject any past-life understanding to ongoing evaluation in the light of the most careful self-scrutiny.

Why bother? If we can't know for sure, what is the value of even trying to know about our past? The answer to this question is one of the best-kept secrets in the field of past-life work: it is not the knowledge of any particular past life that counts. It is instead the personal growth that occurs as we try to gain that knowledge that really matters. With this in mind, let's look at three very important principles that should form the foundation for work with past-life information from any source.

Principle 1: You Will Never Have "Proof" of Accuracy

While it is natural for us to make our first question about any given past life, "How can I know if this past life is true?," we sabotage ourselves when we insist on having this question answered before we go any further.

Stop and think about it for a moment. Do any of us have absolute proof of reincarnation? Of course not. All we have are relative degrees of evidence suggesting that it does. A conviction that reincarnation happens may begin with the sense that the idea just rings true. It may begin with a personal experience that is subjectively convincing. But if we held out for proof that reincarnation was so before we believed in it, there would be no reincarnationists—or at least no intellectually honest re-incarnationists. What we must do (if we are to believe in reincarnation at all) is take a tentative position that reincarnation is most likely true and then let our understanding, experiences, collection of data from books, and so on accumulate over time. Even then, we do not have proof, but rather an accumulation of evidence or support for our belief.

If we cannot hold out for proof about reincarnation, how can we hold out for proof of the validity of any given past life? It is not that the question of proof is a bad one, or that we should play ostrich concerning facts that might disprove a belief about past lives. Certainly, the desire to validate a past-life theory is appropriate, and we should be willing to subject our notions about former incarnations to the kind of scrutiny that will either lead toward or away from support of its truth. But the only way we can do that is to start with those past-life theories that tentatively seem valid—whether because they just "feel right" or because some external evidence supports them—and allow our accumulated experience to add evidence of their truth or to invalidate them. This role of accumulated experience leads to the second important principle.

Principle 2: A "Good" Tentative Past-life Theory Is One That Makes Sense Out of You

The first evaluation criterion to apply to a past life, whether told to you by a psychic, described under hypnosis, or constructed from conscious experience, is, "Does this theory make sense out of some aspect of my current-life experiences or traits?" If it does, then that past-life understanding is worth working with. It may be a literal, historically objective past life. It may be a meaningful personal metaphor. You can't know which, most of the time. But if you are willing to use the insights that come with such a theory, more information will come in due time.

Consider the experience that evolved from one young woman's first regression. Because of strong feelings regarding the French Revolution, she had expected the regression to uncover a life during that tumultuous time. Instead, she found herself describing a life that seemed to be pure fabrication, a kind of mixture of things related to what she consciously knew of the French Revolution and other things that had the flavor of sheer imagination. She saw herself as an Englishwoman from the northern gentry class who was concerned for the welfare of her husband, who was involved in seditious acts. When questioned further, she described the sedition as involving the carrying of secrets back and forth between France and England. This was consistent with what she knew of English involvement with the fate of the French aristocrats, but then she was puzzled to hear herself identifying the threat as coming from King George. The rational monitor within her knew that the English king would not have been a threat at all to those who were trying to help the endangered French aristocracy, and therefore she wanted to dismiss this part of the regression as wrong, even as she said it. The rational monitor was also eager to be precise and was therefore frustrated that no number came when she asked herself, "George the what?" As the story in the regression unfolded, her life seemed to have been largely one of waiting for and worrying about her husband when he was away on his missions. Eventually, he began taking her with him, to give the appearance of innocent family travel to his clandestine trips. Ultimately, they both were arrested, and the regression ended in a scene of great bitterness, with the woman in a dirty jail cell.

When the regression was over, the woman had no

sense that she had come up with anything literally true. To the contrary, she felt quite sure she had made the story up. Yet she was willing to work with this story as a meaningful metaphor about some of her attitudes toward life. She recognized themes of innocence and betrayal, and a certain dynamic between herself and her husband—in which she tended to feel threatened whenever he wanted them to undertake some new experience or endeavor—that was consistent with the story she had woven in her regression. She decided to use those insights to help her be more aware of the ways she was limiting herself through fearful, suspicious, or negative responses to new situations in life.

In being ready to accept at least the symbolic significance of her past-life scenario, the woman created a win-win situation. If she never got anything more than the allegorical help that the story offered, the regression would have served its purpose. On the other hand, it was only her willingness to accept that help that opened the door for validation to come, if indeed she had remembered an actual past life. This leads us to the final principle of past-life work.

Principle 3: The Objective Truth of a Past-life Theory Can Only Be Tested Over Time

Much as we might want to know right away whether we are dealing with fact or fancy, our willingness to grapple with the *lessons* a past-life theory offers is a major factor in determining whether more information comes. In the case of the woman whose story we have been following, that meant applying the symbolic insights from her regression to change the way she responded in certain situations.

It wasn't until a full year later that she happened to pick up a historical novel that dealt with events in England during one of the Jacobite uprisings (circa 1715), a period in history she had previously known nothing about. She found that at that time there had been a shift in the royal family who occupied the English throne, and that while the Hanoverian King George now ruled, many people were loyal to the former rulers, the Stuarts. James Stuart, who would have been King James III of England if he had been allowed to rule, was in exile in France. Those who hoped to see him gain the throne were actively building support for him back home, carrying intelligence concerning their mission back and forth between France and England. To her amazement, she found that the gentry of the north were especially involved in these acts of sedition against King George. And of course, since this was the first George, and he had not yet been succeeded by George II, there was no "I" after his name.

Did the woman now have proof that her regression had uncovered a "real" past life? Not necessarily. It is not out of the question that she had studied this historical period in high school and had tucked those memories away in her unconscious mind. Some might even suggest that she had once seen a movie that took place during these events, or heard someone tell a story or sing a song that related to them. Yet both the book and her regression had gone to a level of detail that was not likely to have been covered in the survey-type world history classes she had taken or in any of the other possible secondhand sources of unconscious knowledge. Furthermore, the question remained: even if she had unconscious knowledge of this period, why had she selected it as the stage for the events in her regression? If she had unconscious memory from studies of this period, she had subconscious knowledge of virtually every era that would be mentioned in a world history course. Why did this particular one surface in her regression?

No, she did not have proof that this past-life scenario

was true. But she certainly had a body of evidence to suggest that it might well be. Over time, it is likely that even more evidence will mount, if this past-life memory continues to be meaningful and she works with it in her daily life. The key, then, is to allow the evidence to unfold as we apply a tentative understanding of our past, and then wait for further information to come. The irony is that the benefit has been derived along the way, in the living and testing of insights. In a very real sense, the arrival at relative sureness about a past life is nothing more than a by-product of a far more important personal growth effort. When we try to establish the sureness before we undertake the growth, we not only put the cart before the horse, but we effectively block the best route to the sureness we so much want.

As in the fable of the hare and the tortoise, the slow and steady approach is sometimes best in the long run. In the next chapter, we will develop a step-by-step plan for past-life discovery that is just such an approach.

10

USING THE EDGAR CAYCE READINGS TO LEARN ABOUT YOUR OWN PAST LIVES

*There are the abilities within each and every entity
to not only recall but to experience that through
which it has passed, as well as that to which it
may attain in the individual experience.*

EDGAR CAYCE reading no. 790–1

PEOPLE ARE OFTEN SURPRISED to hear that
the Edgar Cayce readings can help them get in touch
with their own past lives. After all, what could the legacy
of a psychic who has now been dead for over forty years
possibly tell us about our own former incarnations? We
may readily acknowledge the role that Cayce's 2,500 life
readings have played in reintroducing reincarnation to
Western thinking. We may even have experienced profound changes in our personal outlook because of
Cayce's material on reincarnation. But when it comes to
learning more about our own past lives, we can too
quickly assume that the readings dealt solely with other
people's past experiences and therefore have nothing to
tell us about our own.

Yet, on closer examination, we find that there is still
more to be uncovered in the life readings than the philosophy of reincarnation and the vivid tapestry of our
collective soul history we have examined thus far. If we

look more closely, we can notice a thread that runs through these readings, affirming that each of us can and in fact *do* remember our own past lives. A careful reading of this material will reveal that Edgar Cayce did more than tell people about their prior lives. Again and again he pointed out the ways that they had already been remembering those lives even before they had their readings; and he often gave advice as to how they could enhance that recall and put it to practical use in their lives.

PRINCIPLES OF PAST-LIFE RECALL FROM THE CAYCE READINGS

Edgar Cayce's advice to those who came to him for life readings has general application to us today. In fact, it can become a comprehensive lesson plan for how to become our own best source of past-life understanding. And while it would be doing this rich and multifaceted body of information a grave disservice to reduce it to a cookbook recipe for past-life recall, we can distill from it a series of principles that any one of us can follow to open up our awareness of past-life experiences and their relationship to current-life challenges, problems, and growth issues. Let's consider, then, six key principles of past-life recall that we find in the Cayce readings.

Principle 1: All Have the Capacity to Recall

Even as Cayce met people's requests for psychically obtained past-life information, he seemed gently to nudge them toward awareness of the other avenues of exploration available to them. Repeatedly, he confirmed that their dreams, images that came to them in meditation, and even some waking visions were valid glimpses of the very same past lives that he was describing. After telling one man of a series of lifetimes along the Persian Gulf and northern Africa, a reading added the information that it was scenes from these lives that the man saw in dreams and visions from time to time.

This was quite typical of the way the life readings pointed people toward their own past-life revelations, and it suggests that we might adopt an openness toward our own dreams and visions as valid starting points for past-life research. For example, one contemporary past-life seeker decided to heed this advice and find out what she could about a name that repeated itself to her over and over again as she drifted off to sleep one night. The name turned out to be linked with events in the first-century Christian church, a portion of history that had always fascinated her.

The life readings also lost no opportunity to point out the ways that each person was expressing significant past-life experiences through present personality traits, preferences, fears, and habits. For example, a man who was told of a life in ancient Greece in which he had studied under Socrates was reminded of the strong reasoning power he possessed in his current life.

Even without a reading from Cayce or another psychic, we can trace some of our own traits and fears to past lives hinted at in other portions of our experience. For instance, a young man with a strong, irrational fear of air travel found greater understanding of his fear after a dream in which he saw himself to be a World War II pilot who was shot down.

Cayce often linked the past lives revealed in the readings to peculiar physical and emotional responses that came when circumstances, events, or environmental conditions in this life acted as triggers for unconscious memories. A woman troubled with a tendency to cringe or shudder at words of endearment was better able to understand the source of her reactions when her life reading told of an experience in which she had been so engulfed by others' affections that she lost all sense of self-determination. She had been called "a little angel" in that life because of her sweet acquiescence to others' wishes. No wonder, then, that now her aversion to endearment was strong enough to make her shudder.

In each of these examples from the life readings and from the experiences of contemporary men and women, we can see the workings of memory in the most commonplace human experiences, traits, and reactions. When we stop to consider the literally countless ways that memory can express itself in such daily experiences, we realize that the trick to past-life exploration is not in awakening memory; the memory is already there and functioning to make us the people we are today. Every one of us is a walking, talking past-life memory. As the reading that heads this chapter asserts, "There are the abilities within each and every entity to not only recall but to experience that through which it has passed." The trick, then, is to learn to recognize the unconscious expression of memory and know how to direct this spontaneous and seemingly random flow from the unconscious mind into a more integrated unfolding of memory. The remaining principles will deal with this challenge.

Principle 2: Past-life Recall Begins When You Learn to Recognize Your Unconscious Expressions of Memory

The readings say that our interests come from past experiences that have found "lodgement" within our unconscious minds and are "innately" carried forward in the present. For example, a Cayce reading told one man, who had a great interest in anything pertaining to law and who was prone to dream of desert terrain, that he was once a high sheriff among the early settlers of Arizona.

Even our tastes in furniture and decor, musical instruments, and art can be traced to origins in prior experiences. One woman who tracked down a past life in eighteenth-century England without the benefit of a psychic reading or regression found her taste in furniture and architecture to be an important part of an overall pattern which emerged to suggest many strong connections to that time in Britain. Another woman's seemingly mundane interest in recipe books and clippings was linked in her Cayce reading with a life in which she had found great spiritual truth as a Quaker woman who provided her service to the community through meal preparation. No aspect of personal taste and interest is too commonplace to be considered as a possible past-life carryover. Of course, it would be extreme to suggest that every little aspect of our makeup is deeply significant from the perspective of reincarnation; but entertaining the *possibility* that some aspect of our makeup comes from the past can make the difference between a later breakthrough in memory and a lost opportunity.

Our special empathies and our attraction to particular world cultures reflect the experiences and the settings we have known in the past. A man who was greatly drawn to the Moslem culture and religion was an old Crusader, according to his reading, whose war wounds had been nursed by the very people he had gone to the Holy Land to conquer. If we can become more aware of our own special empathies and attractions, rather than letting them continue to be automatic responses, we will take an important step toward recognizing past-life memory when it happens and paving the way for further insight.

Cayce identified the physical senses as being especially attuned to our unconscious memory. One man was told that his memory of having helped rebuild the wall of Jerusalem was stirred when in this life he encountered odors that he unconsciously associated with that experience. Present-day past-life researchers can take special note of the crucial role that the senses play, and become more aware of memories and emotions that seem to come on the tail of a scent in the breeze. The same contemporary woman who traced a past life in eighteenth-century England found, when she eventually visited the scenes of her suspected past life, that the air was permeated with two scents that had created a deep sense of nostalgic yearning in her since childhood: wild chamomile and boxwood shrubbery.

For other people, hearing, sight, or one of the other senses may provide the dominant entry for past-life associations. One man, whose reading described a life in Egypt in which he had been very active in temple activity, experienced what the reading called "a vibration that has not often been understood" when he heard church bells ringing in his current life. Still another person was told that the view she would behold when looking out of a certain window in the historically preserved town of Williamsburg would be enough to awaken memories from a previous life there.

Even the sight of a single object can trigger floods of memory. The correspondence attached to the life readings includes an account by one man who recalled a strange reaction to a conch shell that he found while walking along a tropical beach with his nurse at the age of four. Greatly taken with the shell, the child asked his nurse what it was. When she told him it was a conch, the man remembers a feeling so foreign to his present life that he momentarily forgot who or where he was. When the voice of his nurse finally brought him out of his reverie, the child's first question was whether people ever have skin the color of conch shells. A simple shell on the beach, and a child's unusual reaction to it. It was only the adult's later memory of the experience that brought speculation about the past-life implications of such an experience, and questions about when and where he might have rather poetically likened someone's skin to the creamy pink of a conch shell. Just so, we must learn to sensitize ourselves to the experiences in this lifetime, both past and present, that awaken strong or unusual responses.

Childhood reactions like the one we have just looked at, which seem to go beyond the range of the child's experience, often open up fruitful lines of exploration. Words and associations out of context with the child's current experience are often a dead giveaway of past-life memory in operation. A woman who received a reading from Edgar Cayce was told of a life in France in which her name had been Lurline. This was the very name, unusual though it was, that she had given a child-hood doll. In my own life, I remember that when I was a small child I would cry out, "Nay! Nay!" when my hair was being washed and I was afraid of getting the water and soap in my eyes. What I meant, of course, was "No! No!" But at the age of two I did not know that "nay" was the archaic form of "no." Even I didn't understand what made me call out what I thought of as the horse's sound, "neigh." What's more, the only time I used that word was during the hair-washing ordeals. I still don't know specifically where this experience fits into a past life, but I have it stored away for future reference when and if more information becomes available.

The habit of filing away unusual experiences for future reference can be indispensable to the successful construction of a past-life theory. Individual clues, which do not seem significant at the time they first surface, often open the door to later understanding. The woman we considered earlier, who has an allergy to the sun, did not consider that physical condition to be important to her understanding of past lives until a series

of other clues pointed to a life among the European
aristocracy of a century or more ago. As she read of the
ladies carrying their parasols to protect their skin from
the sun, her current intolerance of exposure to the sun
took on new meaning. It went beyond the physical carryover that the allergy implied. For the social value system that had placed such a premium on an untanned
skin was shown in all of its transitory shallowness in a
culture where just the opposite—a deep tan—was now
considered "the thing" to have.

These various examples of the ways people have experienced the stirring of sleeping memories through
their traits, emotions, and reactions are just the tip of
the proverbial iceberg. They should, however, give some
idea of the range of life experiences that can be rich
with past-life implications. Most often, these experiences come as isolated glimmers of connection, rather
than as the complete past-life scenarios we might hope
for. The first and most important step we can take, as
the examples above show, is to recognize these experiences as tentatively belonging to the puzzle of our own
past. The next step is to see where that recognition can
lead us.

Principle 3: We Can Make These Isolated
Glimmers from the Past More Complete and
Coherent

Cayce urged us to study the things that quicken our
interest as the means to deeper awakening. Reading
about times, people, and ideas that appeal to us; travel
to parts of the world that call to us; and study of maps,
pictures, and artwork were all recommended as ways to
develop a fledgling past-life memory. A thirteen-year-
old boy whose parents requested a life reading for him
was a religious artist in the early church period, accord-

ing to Cayce. The parents were told that if they would
expose him to Bible story pictures he would not only
respond to them but also would be able to comment on
their accuracy. This exposure would also prime him for
further artistic development in this life, the parents
were told.

Cayce also placed great emphasis on meditation as a
way to enlist the unconscious mind in recall, and encouraged the use of imagination. We may be tempted to
discredit imagination as tantamount to make-believe,
but Cayce seemed to place a higher value on it. What
begins as mere imagination can apparently lead into actual memory. This should be a reminder to us when we
work with regressions or reveries that it is okay to use
active imagination as a jumping-off place. Visualize the
scene of a former life, one woman was told. In another
case, in order to awaken the memory of a meal eaten
with Jesus, parents were advised to ask their daughter,
"What do you suppose was served at that supper?"

Principle 4: Dreams Are a Major Source of Past-life Memory

The life readings repeatedly linked the former incarnations they described to dreams that the recipients had
already experienced before the life reading was given.
And when people asked about the meaning of their
dreams, past-life implications were often brought out.

This can serve as a reminder to us not to underesti-
mate the importance of dreams as a source of past-life
insight. When we remember that dreams are nightly excursions into the very levels of consciousness where
past-life memories are stored, it is easy to see why this
valuable source of insight should not be overlooked in
any comprehensive approach to past-life understanding.
Also, because dreams tend to come as a commentary on

current issues, attitudes, behaviors, and situations in waking life, the past-life memories that stir in your dream memory are going to be especially significant for your growth here and now.

Nonetheless, we frequently overlook past-life dreams simply because we do not know how to recognize them when they come. How does a past-life dream differ from an ordinary dream? Some are easily recognizable because they have the look and feel of a trip backward in time. For example, they may involve the following:

- scenery or a setting that looks like another time period, a foreign part of the world, or a culture other than one's own
- characters (often including you, the dreamer) wearing the garb of another time or culture, or bearing distinct physical traits of a race other than the dreamer's current race
- the speaking of recognizable or unrecognizable foreign languages
- dream plots involving historical events, such as major wars, cultural achievements, religious developments, or natural disasters

Most often, however, past-life clues are woven in among otherwise contemporary dreams. These may go unnoticed if we do not know what to look for. Any one —or combination—of the following *may* be signals that the dream is reflecting past-life connections to current-life situations:

- You may dream of finding items from the past, such as old coins, jewelry, pottery shards, tools, or books.
- Your dream images may have names that suggest references to other countries or cultures. For example, the appearance of *French* doors, an *In-*

dian blanket, an *Italian* sculpture, a *Greek* vase, or an *Egyptian* scarab amidst other dream symbols that are more familiar in your waking life may be a cue alerting you to connect the story of the dream with a past-life setting in the country represented by the more exotic image.

• When you or someone known to you in waking life takes a changed identity or role in your dream, it may be due to unconscious past-life memory. If a dream character is male in the dream, but female in waking life; white in the dream, but black in waking life; dark-haired in the dream, but light-haired in waking life (to give just a few examples), you may be experiencing yourself or the other person as he or she actually was in a former appearance. Similarly, if the person who is now a spouse appears in the dream as a child or a sibling, the dream may be suggesting past-life relationship roles that differ from the present.

Admittedly, it is sometimes difficult to separate past-life dreams from regular dreams. The very nature of a past-life dream is that it shows the blending and carrying over of issues from one life to another. However, if you will *experiment* with the past-life connection that a dream *might* be showing, further dreams and waking experiences will help you determine whether you are facing a literal past-life memory or a past-life metaphor that helps make sense out of a current situation.

If past-life clues come up in your dreams, you can be sure it is because growth issues that you have come into this life to work on are coming up in your waking experience. Past-life exploration and dream exploration work in a cooperative circle. The more you pay attention to your dreams in general, the more likely it is that past-life information will emerge in your dreams. And the more you work *consciously* to develop your best understanding of past-life connections to current-life situations, the more you will encourage and be able to recognize past-life information in your dreams when it does come.

Principle 5: The Right Purposes Will Help Memory

As we have already seen, the readings' approach to past-life exploration is inseparably tied to issues of personal and spiritual growth. Those few people who were discouraged from digging into their past were warned about getting sidetracked from their spiritual purposes. The majority, who were encouraged to pursue greater understanding of their past, were reminded of the kind of purposes that tied the endeavor to their personal and spiritual growth:

- awakening strengths, abilities, and positive personal qualities from the past
- understanding and overcoming fears and problems that linger from prior experiences
- clarification of soul purpose. One woman was told that greater knowledge of her many lives would help her to see that all material life is an expression of God. Another was told that her experience in past-life recall would serve as an example to awaken others to spiritual truth and power.

Principle 6: Past-life Understanding Cannot Be Rushed

Finally, and perhaps most important, the readings' encouragement to pursue and explore the past was tempered with the reminder that memories must be allowed to unfold in their own time. As we have already considered in the last chapter, the process of unfoldment is the important part of past-life work. Also, even though we may be impatient to get the whole story, our understanding and our readiness to deal with the past must keep pace with the memories that awaken.

The approach to past-life work outlined here might be described as a "safe" approach because it does take this all-important factor into account. There is little to be gained and much to be lost in forcing the issue before we are ready to handle it, when it comes to some of the pain and trauma that is inevitably a part of the past. As one Cayce reading put it, "the consciousness [of past-life experiences] takes the individual where it is; not where it desires to be!" It should come as a comfort rather than a frustration, then, that past-life knowledge tends to develop gradually. When we are willing to approach it from this perspective, there is no limit to the insights and growth in store for us.

Part IV

REINCARNATION AND THE WAY OF GRACE

What is karmic debt? This ye have made a bugaboo! This ye have overbalanced within thyself! What is thy life but the gift of thy Maker that ye may be wholly one with Him?
EDGAR CAYCE reading no. 1436–3

11

THE INEXHAUSTIBLE LOVE OF GOD

To be sure, law applies. For in the beginning of man, in his becoming a living soul in the earth, laws were established and these take hold. But lose not sight of the law of grace, the law of mercy, the law of patience as well.

EDGAR CAYCE reading no. 2977–2

WHILE IT IS IMPORTANT to understand what the theory of reincarnation can tell us about ourselves and our lives, such a focus does not bring out the whole story of our experience as souls. Indeed, if we look only at what reincarnation tells us about why we are the way we are and why things happen as they do in our lives, we miss a very important aspect of this philosophy as presented in the Cayce readings. For, in the deepest sense, the story of reincarnation is not about us at all. It is about our Creator and his unfailing love for us. It is about nothing less than an entire universe unfolding for our greatest good and growth. Finally, it is about the *grace* that is freely offered to all who are willing to accept it.

What is grace? For some, the term grace is laden with specific religious or even denominational connotations. For others, it is an enigma. For still others, it is a too-good-to-be-true promise of an easy way out.

The dictionary defines grace as "the free and unmerited love and favor of God." As treated in the Cayce material, grace is an actual spiritual law that expresses such divine qualities as love, mercy, patience, and forgiveness; it is also a law that has great bearing on the process of reincarnation. In fact, no discussion of the readings' version of the philosophy of reincarnation would be complete without a careful look at grace; for Cayce deals with this law as a central aspect of the relationship between God and humanity, and even as an alternative to karma.

The readings' emphasis on grace tells us that karma is not the only means of bringing confused, wayward, and often rebellious souls home. It tells us that even as the soul makes its journey through earthly existence under the guidance of the law of karma, that journey can be aided, cushioned, or completely transformed at any time through the law of grace. It tells us of a love strong enough to work miracles in our hearts and in our experience—if the soul chooses to accept the way of grace, that is.

What *is* the way of grace? How can grace, the "free, unmerited love and favor of God," be a law? And what does it have to do with karma? Any readers who are a bit bewildered about these and other questions concerning grace should not feel alone. The workings of grace may well be one of the ultimate mysteries of life. As such, it defies neat definitions and pat explanations. It may be accurate to say that grace is something we can come to *apprehend,* but never fully *comprehend;* that is, we may come into an awareness of grace even while the intellect remains somewhat baffled as to what grace really is. For this reason, I would like to approach the mystery we call grace obliquely—by first exploring our capacity to become aware of it, and then by attempting to construct some systematic understanding of what grace is and how it works in our lives.

THE AWARENESS OF GRACE

The direct awareness of grace—what I have called apprehending it—sometimes comes upon us spontaneously, like a happy surprise or realization. When this happens, we have usually stumbled upon a profound sense of how the love and mercy of God manifests itself in human experience. One Cayce reading aptly describes this spontaneous awareness of grace as a sudden experience of "harmony and beauty and grace" that causes us to wonder what moved us to feel different in that moment (no. 3098–2). We may experience such a moment on a spring morning, when the new life all around us affirms that life is good after all; or on a cold winter evening, when home is warm and cozy. These are the moments that go beyond happiness or pleasure or even contentment; they are brief moments when the external and internal worlds meet in harmony and we catch a glimpse of the ultimate goodness of life; and they are reminders to us that we are a part of that harmony. In such moments we experience grace, even if we cannot define it.

The awareness of grace is also triggered sometimes during moments of need, such as when we pray for a sick loved one and, against all odds, she recovers. Or when we reach the limits of our capacity to cope with something in our lives, call out to God in desperation, and then feel the indescribable sense of the burden becoming lighter. Such are the more dramatic awakenings to grace.

Grace tugs at our awareness in the smaller crises of life, too. For example, even though our mind has wandered for a moment as we drive down a busy road, we somehow manage to avoid another car or a bicyclist who suddenly appears in our path. Or when, even though we carelessly lose a wallet or some prized pos-

session, it is found and returned to us. At these times
there is a special awareness behind our gratitude that
tells us we really are not alone, that there *is* someone or
something out there looking after us. This, too, is an
example of what the direct apprehension of grace can
feel like.

These experiences that usher in the sense that we
have somehow been blessed, protected, or touched by
something beyond ourselves—something that is good—
are but a few of the kind of experiences that bring us
closer to apprehending grace in our lives.

The contexts in which grace can come upon us are as
varied as we are, and so it would be pointless to try to
catalog the literally countless experiences that can trigger an awareness of grace. But however varied might be
the experiences, they tend to have a common quality:
vulnerability. Sometimes the vulnerability comes when
we have been pushed so close to the edge of destruction
(physically, emotionally, or spiritually) that all of our
defenses are down. Sometimes the vulnerability comes
because we know that we have been wrong or negligent
in some way. Sometimes the vulnerability is merely an
openness to something beyond ourselves, a willingness
to be touched on a deep level by beauty, truth, or compassion for another human being. Whatever the form
our vulnerability may take, it seems to create a moment
when self steps out of the way long enough for God's
love to take over. This kind of vulnerability is largely a
spontaneous reaction. As such, it cannot be induced.

But while we cannot induce the spontaneous vulnerability that opens the way for grace to flow in and meet
the need of the moment, we *can* create a context in our
lives and in our thinking that welcomes grace rather
than rebuffs it. This is a different kind of vulnerability.
It is a matter of acknowledging the ways in which our
philosophies and our lives are not complete without
grace. It means at times sacrificing the smug sense of

self-sufficiency and allowing much-needed aid to flow into our lives. It is also a matter of expectancy—acknowledging the ways that grace can transform some of life's most troubling experiences into encounters with God's love and mercy. Simply put, it is the recognition of how much we *need* grace—not only during specific crises, but as part of our outlook on life.

If we can bring an awareness of the importance of grace to our thinking, then we are that much more likely to experience it when those spontaneous moments of need arise. Especially when we hold a reincarnationist worldview, which is influenced so strongly by an understanding of the law of karma, it is important that we stop and consider the equal importance of grace. For, as we shall now see, there are pitfalls inherent in a personal philosophy based on karma *without* grace.

WHY KARMA ALONE IS NOT ENOUGH

Karma is good. That we can affirm. As an expression of the perfect and harmonious force behind this universe, it can only *be* good. The law of karma brings to us the very experiences we need, and an understanding of the law of karma helps us meet those experiences as constructively as possible. It is good, then, to incorporate karma into our thinking. But we find in the Cayce readings the principle that anything that has the potential to help also has the potential to harm. Human nature usually wants to protest this idea and assert that if a little of something is good, a lot must be even better. Yet the readings repeatedly say that we should strive for moderation. Too much of even a good thing can become harmful.

This idea is expressed most concretely in the health readings, which insist that the very presence of curative power in a substance should warn us that it holds the opposite potential as well—if it is used improperly or used in excess. It is expressed more abstractly in the statement elsewhere in the readings that evil is only good that has been misused. The same principle is certainly true with respect to the law of karma. If we take karma to extremes in our thinking, we can misapply it to life's situations. As a result of such "karmic thinking" (as we shall call it), we can unwittingly limit and hold ourselves back in some crucial ways.

In our consideration of the law of consequences in chapter six, for example, we looked at the fallacy of assuming that karmic action is always the explanation for life's hardships. We saw how such an assumption can cause us to misjudge others and castigate ourselves. At those times, having karma in our thinking becomes a stumbling block to our growth rather than the help it is meant to be. As we shall now see, there are other situations in which the knowledge of karma, untempered with the knowledge of grace, can lead us to jump to some conclusions about life that are not necessarily valid or growth-promoting. Before we look at these grace-inhibiting headsets, I want to stress that it is not that karma is sometimes good for us and other times bad for us, or that a little bit of karma is good while a lot is bad. My point, rather, is about how much we *think* of karma when trying to understand life's experiences.

Although it is generally helpful to have an understanding of karma as part of our outlook on life, an obsessive, "tunnel vision" approach to karma can have a detrimental effect. With this distinction in mind, then, let's look at some of the things that can happen when our thinking is so dominated with principles of cause and effect that we are not able to see other possibilities.

Fatalism

We can lapse into a fatalistic view of life. As we've already seen in examining free will and so-called karmic destiny, we are limited to some degree by past choices that have determined the options facing us in any given moment. We cannot ignore the formative power of past choices. But the fatalism that says, "It's my karma," when some disagreeable thing happens, can be paralyzing. It robs us of the God-given right—and mandate—to choose anew in each moment. It even blinds us to the love of God that *wants* us to be free. Worse yet, the fatalism that looks across the world at starving people or back in history to massacred people and says, "It's their karma," indicates a sealed-off and hardened outlook devoid of compassion. Is there a frame of mind more likely to produce "bad karma" than indifference to others' suffering? And what consciousness could be more closed to the love and mercy of God than one that assumes there is no choice but to endure hardship?

A fatalistic outlook can seem very spiritual, in that it suggests a willingness to accept life's disappointments and put self-will aside. But if we're not careful, it can also allow us to become metaphysical automatons who are so busy accepting what we assume to be "the will of the universe" that we forget to interact with life. We forget to take on the challenge of making ourselves and the world around us better. When we take fatalism to its extreme, we forget to grow—and then we lose the whole point of being in the earth. It is important, then, that we not let an acceptance of the law of cause and effect blind us to the moment-by-moment freedom and responsibility of choice. The Creator who has given us life in the earth as an opportunity to grow does not want us to have to face our challenges with one hand tied behind our backs, but rather with all of the resources of a fully choosing child of God.

Paradoxically, however, even this necessary claiming of responsibility for making choices can lead us into trouble if we're not balanced in our approach. Just as a too-intense focus on cause and effect can lead some people into the paralysis of inaction, it can lead others into an exhausting pursuit of perfection. This leads us to the second drawback of karmic thinking.

"I Must Save Myself"

We can labor under the burden of believing we must save ourselves. Unlike the person who lapses into fatalistic thinking, the person who steps into the opposite pitfall says, "Yes, I know I'm in control. I know I'm responsible to choose and create only the best conditions in my life. Only I can make myself perfect; no one else can do it for me. I must save myself." And so begins an effort at self-perfection that sabotages many a well-meaning spiritual seeker.

How does this sabotage occur? As we invest our all in the project of becoming perfect, inevitably our progress is uneven. Sometimes we are fairly successful at putting our spiritual ideals into practice; other times we fail miserably. As we alternate between success and failure, thinking all the time that we are involved in a solo effort to become perfect, we can bounce back and forth between spiritual pride and spiritual despair. Both states of mind—one a misguided self-sufficiency and the other a plummet into despondent inadequacy—are anything but conducive to true spiritual growth.

For example, a subtle egotism can creep in just when we observe the positive signs of cause and effect in our lives. If money matters are flowing well and you have been trying to give freely, in cooperation with the law of positive return, it is easy to say, "I am experiencing abundance because that's what is due me. I deserve it." Or if your personal relationships develop harmoniously just as you are working very hard at practicing the Golden Rule, your private thoughts might whisper to you, "You're really a nicer, more caring person than most other people. It's understandable that people like you so much." Even though we rarely give voice to such self-congratulating thoughts, it is difficult not to think them when cause and effect dominates our thinking. For when we see cause and effect as the sole expression of divine law, it is only logical to conclude that good fortune comes as the reward for and testimony to our spiritual accomplishment. Such conclusions lead naturally to spiritual conceit.

"What's wrong with feeling good about yourself?" you may be asking. Nothing at all—provided that your ability to feel good about yourself does not depend completely on how well you've been doing lately in your efforts to be spiritual (or your efforts at anything else, for that matter). Spiritual conceit is *not* the same thing as positive self-regard. Positive self-regard is a matter of loving oneself because the self is perceived as worthy of love. Spiritual egotism is a matter of loving oneself for all the wrong reasons. Like the demanding parent who only loves the child when he brings home A's on his report card, spiritual egotists love themselves when their performance is up to the proper standard.

By contrast, healthy self-love does not exist because of performance; it sometimes even exists in *spite* of it. We may take pleasure in living right, just the way the truly loving parent may delight in the child's good school performance. But healthy self-love does not derive its justification from acts of spiritual virtue. To do so is just another form of identifying with our creations rather than with who we really are. And when we derive our sense of worth from acts of spiritual virtue, we slip into what the Cayce readings call self-aggrandizement, one of the shortcomings most frequently warned against.

Why is the spiritual conceit that Cayce called self-aggrandizement so dangerous? For one thing, when spiritual egotism takes over, we take credit for life's blessings, rather than give thanks for them. Such response doesn't leave very much room for communion with the Creator whose love has made it all possible. Neither does it leave much room for love of self when our spiritual virtue slips a bit. Here is where the plummet into despondency begins.

When we love ourselves the way God loves us, positive performance under the law of karma is not the *reason* for the love. Therefore the love remains even when we recognize that the performance is not all that it might be. But when we take so much pride in our spiritual virtue that we claim credit for the blessings in our lives, just the opposite happens when things go wrong. Self-blame and self-accusation take over. We cannot love ourselves and we cannot believe in God's love for us. At those times we know the isolation that comes with trying to save ourselves. We know the desolation that comes with undertaking the mammoth task of self-perfection without an advocate to help carry the load. We know what it's like to try to grow without the light of God's love to help us along the way.

So it can go when karmic thinking prevails in our personal philosophy. We bounce back and forth between spiritual pride and guilt. Through it all, the emphasis is on self—self's successes and self's failures—rather than on the sustaining presence of God and our Oneness with him. When karma exists without grace, there is no way to succeed other than by becoming perfect. Every shortcoming must be overcome by the sweat of our own effort. Every mistake must be paid for. This latter assumption has its own paralyzing effect, as we shall now see.

"It'll Catch Up with Me Someday"

We can be dogged by the uneasy thought that everything we've done wrong will someday catch up with us. I call this the "It'll catch up with me someday" syndrome. Most reincarnationists who have lapsed into purely karmic thinking know what this feels like. You're sailing along in life, doing fairly well in living up to your spiritual ideals, and things are going smoothly, but in the back of your mind is something you did "wrong" some time back. It may have been a major infraction against your sense of right and wrong; it may have been something relatively small. But whatever the original guilt-provoking act was, even after you no longer feel actively guilty about it, you believe that someday, in some way, that particular piece of karma is going to catch up with you. It may be three lifetimes from now. You may be living the most spiritual of lives, cooperating with every higher law that you know about; and something you did in 1975 will come due, and that's when the bottom will fall out.

How many conscientious spiritual seekers live with that ghost? When karma alone makes up our understanding, we live with the gnawing conviction that we are eventually going to have to meet everything we've ever done. Like death and taxes, "karmic debt" takes its place beside the things we know we must face someday, but not just yet. It gets added to the baggage that we carry with us through life—sometimes as part of our conscious worry load, but more often lurking beyond the edges of consciousness and merely weighing us down. Is it really necessary to carry this load? Not when we add grace to our understanding of how reincarnation works. It *is* true that we will have to meet everything we've ever done, but the law of grace promises that it does not have to be in the ways that we most fear. For under the influence of grace, even the most dreaded of life's experiences can be transformed into encounters with God's love and mercy. Yet if karma alone is in our thinking, we may never realize this transformative power of grace.

The extremes of karmic thinking—the assumption that "someone is being punished," fatalism, the exhausting and seemingly impossible pursuit of self-perfection, and the "It'll catch up with me someday" syndrome—all arise out of personal philosophies that are based on karma alone. Each in its own way limits our growth and impairs our flexibility in dealing with life. Each also reflects the influence of karma without the tempering influence of grace. To put it another way, each one of these attitudes overlooks what can happen when the love of God predominates in our expectations.

THE LOVE OF GOD

One of the main appeals of the philosophy of reincarnation is its assertion of God's fairness. What a relief it is when we add reincarnation to the puzzling picture of human suffering! God is not causing little children in Africa to starve, and he's not to blame for the countless lives lost in wars. Nor is he responsible for the unkind turns of fate that seem to cast heartache randomly upon the human race. When we learn that choices among souls bring these things on, we eagerly embrace explanations that reassert our desperate hope that God is fair.

Yet, because of this very emphasis on the fairness of God, the philosophy of reincarnation sometimes makes him into an inexorable force of justice—blind justice that cannot bend the rules in response to human pleas for mercy and forgiveness, because the law of cause and effect cannot be denied. We can see how, under the influence of thinking that is oriented solely toward justice, God all too easily becomes an unbending, unmerciful, unloving force. Reconciliation with him is certainly possible, and even promised; but only after we have mended our ways, only after we have shown ourselves worthy of his love and have reinstated ourselves into a condition of harmony with him.

But in the Cayce readings' story of reincarnation, the justice of God does not require that every debt be paid. It requires only that we learn the difference between right and wrong and revise our thoughts and actions accordingly. Sometimes we learn that difference when the force of karma puts us back on track; but we may also learn that difference at any time through the force of God's grace in our lives. The choice is ours. In the next chapter, we will take a look at when and how we can make that choice, and how it can change the course of our lives when we do.

12
BETWEEN KARMA AND GRACE

*Then as the entity sets itself to do or to accomplish
that which is of a creative influence or force, it
comes under the interpretation of the law between
karma and grace. No longer is the entity then
under the law of cause and effect, or karma . . .*
                    EDGAR CAYCE reading no. 2800–2

MANY PEOPLE EXPERIENCE GRACE every day,
but have never thought to call it that. On the other
hand, many others may have experienced precious little
grace, simply because they are holding on to assumptions that act as barriers to the flow of grace into their
lives. One thing is fairly certain: all of us make choices
between karma and grace every day of our lives. Much
of the time those choices are automatic, part of our
habitual response patterns to life's situations. But if we
can learn to recognize the openings for grace to enter
human experience, we not only deepen our understanding of this mystery called grace, we also learn to make
more grace-oriented choices. Let's look at some hypothetical past-life scenarios that illustrate key distinctions
between karma and grace.

Six Past-life Scenarios

Scenario 1a. Marcus was an early Roman born into the
patrician class. He had a powerful intellect, was extremely ambitious, and had a natural talent for leader-

ship. In his early life, he rose through a series of government positions that gave him ever-increasing power until one day he was finally in line to become a praetor, one of the most powerful positions in the republic. However, Marcus soon became aware that he had an enemy in the Assembly who would oppose his election and sway others to do likewise.

In a fever of consuming ambition, Marcus arranged the assassination of his political enemy. Once this enemy was out of the way, Marcus was elected. His love of power continued to grow, and by the time of his death in that lifetime he had become totally corrupt.

In a later incarnation, this soul appears to be a born loser. His career moves and his personal relationships alike always end in disaster. He spends much of his life feeling frustrated and downtrodden, and ultimately takes his own life.

Scenario 1b. Gaius was another Roman patrician whose political rise took him right to the brink of praetorship. He, too, learned of a political enemy in the Senate and plotted an assassination. But before he could carry out his intentions, Gaius was struck with the horror of the crime he was about to commit. He decided that his political ambition was not worth another man's life, and consequently abandoned his plans for murder.

Gaius never did rise to the rank of Roman praetor, but in a subsequent life he is once again a born leader. From high school student council to corporate power structure, the soul who used to be Gaius quickly wins the confidence and support of his peers. Eventually, he is elected mayor of his midsized city.

Scenario 2a. Maggie was a young woman who became pregnant out of wedlock in Victorian England. Unable to face her shame, she slipped away to London, where the baby was born. Knowing that her life would be ruined if anyone found out about her illegitimate child, Maggie left the infant on a London doorstep one dark winter night. She never knew whether the child lived or died or, if it lived, what kind of life it had.

In the next life, the soul who was Maggie is born out of wedlock and quickly abandoned. She grows up in an assortment of orphanages and foster homes, never knowing the love and security of a real family.

Scenario 2b. Dorothy was another young woman in Victorian England who found herself in a situation similar to Maggie's. Like Maggie, she fled to the anonymity of the city, abandoned her child on a doorstep soon after it was born, and resumed her life, never knowing the fate of the child.

In her next life, the soul who had been Dorothy is greatly drawn to social work, especially where children are concerned. She eventually becomes the dedicated head of an orphanage in her city.

Scenario 3a. Ned was a ruthless slave overseer in pre-Civil War Georgia. He worked his slaves to the point of exhaustion, and was without mercy when one of them violated his rigid rules.

In his next life, this soul is born black in Mississippi in the 1930s. He must endure the scorn of white people and the indignity of the Jim Crow laws. His life is one of poverty, bitterness, and despair.

Scenario 3b. Abel was also a slave overseer, on a South Carolina plantation in the mid-1800s. His treatment of the slaves was no better than Ned's. He took pride in being hated and feared by every slave in the county.

In his next life, Abel is also born black in Mississippi in the 1930s. But unlike Ned, Abel finds himself sparked into action by the inhumanity of the discrimination he is expected to endure. By the time he reaches adulthood, this former slave overseer becomes an articulate and effective leader in the civil rights movement.

What Happened?

In each pair of life stories above, the same initial situation led to two very different outcomes. What was the difference between Marcus and Gaius? Both had the same talents, ambitions, opportunities, and temptations. Yet one's experience led to his downfall, while the other's paved the way for fulfillment. In the case of Maggie and Dorothy, each chose preservation of her pride and her role in society over the welfare of her child. Yet one seems to be paying for it, while the other "got off." Ned and Abel both incurred the same "karmic debt," and both in fact landed in life situations that reflected their karma. But Ned's was a life of misery, while Abel's was one of dignity and achievement.

How is it that Gaius, Dorothy, and Abel fared so much better than Marcus, Maggie, and Ned? Can it be that the law of karma metes out worse fates to some than to others? Or was there rather some fundamental difference in how the souls in each pair reacted to their experience? The answer to this question may be found in the law of grace, and our understanding of where it fits into the soul's ongoing chain of choices and experiences. For in each of the scenarios above, we have seen souls choosing between karma and grace. In order to understand those choices more fully, let's look at what we *can* know about the workings of the law of grace.

THE PARADOX OF GRACE

The most basic definition of grace, as we have already seen, is "the free, unmerited love and favor of God." That means we don't have to do anything to earn it. In fact, we *can't* earn it. The grace that flows from God to us has nothing to do with our worthiness. It is there in the darkest moments of our lives, and it is there during times of greatest spiritual awakening. It is there for the criminal on death row, and it is there for the nun who prays in the convent. In our scenarios above, it was there for Marcus as well as Gaius, for Maggie as well as Dorothy, and for Ned as well as Abel. It is always there. It *must* always be there, because it emanates from God's very nature. Our job is not to earn it, but to open up to it. Therein lies the great paradox surrounding the law of grace: it is an unearned gift.

Grace: The Unearned Gift

Grace is the unearned gift that we must nonetheless accept before we can receive it. It is all too easy to think that grace is something that we must make happen. In considering the sample scenarios, for example, it is tempting to conclude that those with the happier endings to their stories were somehow more virtuous or worked more constructively with the law of cause and effect. Yet the minute we approach grace as something we can create or as a law that we can *manipulate,* we block the flow of that grace and actually keep it from reaching us.

Grace is a gift we can allow and receive, but we can never summon it. In fact, there is no need to summon it —for it is always there, unfolding in its own time and way. It requires our cooperation, but not our interference. If we are like the impatient child who keeps digging up seeds in the garden to see if they are growing, we will most certainly halt the unfolding of grace in our lives.

Grace comes completely from God's side of the relationship between creature and Creator. Yet even a cursory look around will tell us that grace does not appear to be dispensed evenly. Some people seem to flourish in the sunlight of God's love and blessings, while others

have never known what it is like to feel the love of God
in their hearts. Half of the people in the sample scenarios experienced grace, the other half did not. Even in
more traditional evangelical Christian understandings,
where grace saves the soul despite human unworthiness,
only some people seem to be able to muster up the faith
that is necessary in order to claim that grace.

Is God capricious, giving some the power to experience grace and denying it to others? It would seem far
more consistent with a God who loves all of his children
equally to think that there is *some* vital part we play,
something we must do, which makes the difference between experiencing grace and not experiencing it. As we
shall see shortly, that "something" is simply a matter of
choosing to open up to grace at any one of three stages
in our experience with a difficult situation.

Karma and Grace

Karma and grace are two sides to the same reality. Life
is made up of polarities: male/female, right brain/left
brain, analytical/intuitive, active/passive, giving/receiv-
ing, logical/irrational. These are but a few of the polarities by which contemporary psychology and metaphysics
have come to describe the range of human experience.
In the light of what we find as we look deeply into the
Cayce reincarnation readings, karma and grace make up
one more set of polarities that apply to the soul's experience. They are opposite sides of the same coin, and
together they lead us into harmony with the same reality
—the soul's Oneness with God.

Here again, we find paradox. Karma and grace are
not the same law. Their workings may take the soul
along distinctly different paths, as we shall see. Our sub-
jective experience under grace is often totally unlike
that which we experience under karma. Yet both karma

and grace spring from the love of God. Both work only good in our lives, in that they are natural forces in this universe that move us toward greater harmony with the ultimate harmony, love, and Oneness that is God. If we were to depict the journey of the soul in images of a long road, the road labeled "karma" and the road labeled "grace" would both lead to the same destination. But the road of karma would be the tougher road, dark in places, strewn with obstacles and twisted with detours. The road of grace would be sunlit and pleasant by comparison.

Yet here the analogy breaks down. For karma and grace are not really two distinct roads representing separate pathways to God. Nor is karma the "bad guy" in a "good guy–bad guy" dichotomy. The law of cause and effect is not just a bad-tasting medicine that ultimately helps us be good. It also brings good things into our lives, as we saw when we considered the law of continuation and the law of positive return. Karma and grace are one, just as the head side and the tail side are still one coin. The way of grace cannot obliterate the law of cause and effect, nor does cause and effect operate outside of the loving influence of god's grace.

If I sound as if I am contradicting myself here, I am—in a way. That is the nature of paradox. Two ideas, each true, seem mutually exclusive. But that is only how it looks from the limited perspective of physical consciousness. There is a higher reality where the polarities of spiritual paradoxes blend into one. From the perspective of earthly life, karma and grace are separate laws and we tend to experience them as such. Therefore we will consider them as separate, as alternatives that we can choose. From a higher perspective, however, they are one expression of the same loving God. This leads us to consider one final paradox, which paves the way for discussion of the all-important question: how do we go about letting grace enter our lives?

Grace Supersedes Karma

From the perspective that sees karma and grace as separate laws, we might describe grace as having the power to supersede karma without contradicting it. The reading that heads this chapter, for instance, refers to the possibility of "no longer being under the law of cause and effect." Does this mean that grace does away with the necessity that we think and act in ways that are consistent with the goodness of this universe? Do what you want to do and God will forgive you? Hardly.

The possibility of grace entering our lives does not depend on whether God can overlook our shortcomings. To the contrary, it requires not only God but us as well looking them squarely in the eye. Never are we made to face our faults more uncompromisingly than when we are in the presence of grace. If such a thought is surprising or seems inconsistent with the loving quality of grace, perhaps we can find a parallel in one of the most frequently reported elements of near-death experiences.

Time and time again, people who have been clinically dead and subsequently revived tell of meeting a being of light. This being knows them completely and isn't blinking at their mistakes along the way in life. They know that this being is fully aware of the worst things about them and in this being's presence they are even compelled to see their most hidden sins. And yet this being of light loves them with a love that surpasses anything they have known on earth. This being sees their shortcomings and yet doesn't think any less of them for it. This being's love is truly unconditional. It does not depend on their worthiness.

The grace of God has that quality. It holds us fully accountable without condemning. In fact, it brings us into *greater* accountability, greater awareness of our shortcomings, to prime us for the change in consciousness that grace entails. We have not yet defined grace as a change in consciousness, but this, too, is one of its many facets. It is a change in consciousness that can soften the blows of karmic results, transform our deepest urges and motivations in life so that we live more cooperatively with karma in the first place, and actually alter the course of our soul's experience so that we no longer have to meet our karma under the rigors of the law of consequences.

Sound too good to be true? Doesn't the law of cause and effect require that we reap everything that we have sown? Yes, it does. But there is more than one way to reap, to come to terms with our mistakes. The law of grace becomes far more consistent with what we know about the undeniability of the law of cause and effect when we stop and remind ourselves what the true purpose of karma is. That purpose is *not* to punish wrongdoing. The purpose of the law of cause and effect is, rather, educational: to teach us to live in harmony with the laws of the universe. The immutable aspect of the law requires that we learn from our mistakes—not that we be punished for them. It doesn't matter whether we learn life's lessons through the school of hard knocks or through a change of heart, a change of understanding. We have opportunity at any time to "wake up" to our own Oneness with God on the deepest level; and, at the same time, to wake up to the forgiveness that is already extended to us. It is then that grace may slip in and surprise us.

RECOGNIZING THE OPPORTUNITIES FOR GRACE

At first glance, there seems to be very little system in the way the Cayce readings talk about grace. In one context grace seems to be an attitude or state of mind that the seeker must hold, while in another grace seems to be a dispensation from God. Some readings recommend grace as a means to keep us on the path toward wholeness and Oneness with God; others present grace as the love that welcomes us back after we have strayed from that path. It can be very confusing, until we realize that this assortment of references to grace *does* form a pattern.

If we look more closely, we find that grace can come into our lives in several distinct ways, depending on how soon we "wake up" to it—thus the seeming hodgepodge of references to it in the Cayce readings. The grace itself, as a constant law emanating from God's love and mercy, will always have the same basic qualities to it that we have already considered. But just as the law of cause and effect can take several different paths, depending on our choices, the law of grace manifests differently depending on our choices with respect to it. In essence, it is a matter of whether we open up to grace before, during, or after the moments of decision that have the potential to set off negative cause-and-effect chains in our lives.

Interestingly enough, beyond the basic definition cited earlier—"the free unmerited love and favor of God"—the dictionary's definition also includes several shades of meaning that roughly correspond to the different ways the Cayce readings refer to the law of grace: "divine influence acting in man to restrain him from sin; a state of reconciliation with God; and spiritual instruction, improvement, edification." Each of these definitions, when considered alongside the Cayce readings and the sample scenarios already introduced, clarify how and when we can choose grace.

Making the Right Choices

Grace can save us from making the choices that must eventually bring on the corrective action of karma. This is the aspect of grace that, in the more traditional theological terminology of the dictionary, is called a "divine influence acting in man to restrain him from sin." If we translate those words into concepts more consistent with the framework we have been using, we might say that this aspect of grace works on our motivations to make us choose those things that are in harmony with the deepest ideal of Oneness and love. The Cayce readings refer to grace in this mode as being a spiritual force that directs the ideals of each soul-entity.

It is this action of grace that we see in the contrasting scenarios of Marcus and Gaius. Marcus allowed his ambition to become the overriding motivation of his life. His choices reflected that, and set a string of karmic effects in motion. Gaius, also very ambitious, came close to making the same choice that Marcus made. For a while, he too was ready to let his desire for position and power cause him to take another human being's life. But he had a change of heart before he could carry out his assassination plot, and thus Gaius ended up setting a very different kind of cause in motion.

How is this any different from what we have already learned about karma? Don't the stories of Marcus and Gaius merely illustrate the difference between souls choosing "good karma" and souls choosing "bad karma"? Where is the grace in this situation?

To answer the last question first, the grace entered Gaius's experience when he had a sudden change of heart regarding his intended act of murder. At that moment, a soul who had been motivated by his own selfish power drives became aware of a higher good—and changed his behavior accordingly. Why must we call this

Figure 1   Grace Intervening Before a Negative Choice

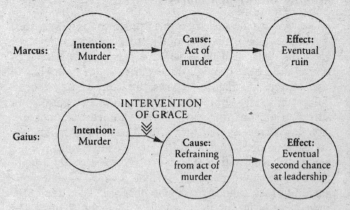

grace? Why can't we just give Gaius the credit for making a good choice? Worse yet, if we can't give Gaius the credit for doing the right thing, but must instead attribute his actions to grace, must we not then give God the blame for Marcus's doing the wrong thing?

We can give Gaius credit for allowing an opening in his heart and consciousness so that grace could flow in, but remember the paradox: we do not earn grace, and yet the responsibility to open up to it falls on our own shoulders. Opening up to the influence of grace is exactly what Marcus did not do. Gaius had to allow the influence of grace to enter consciousness, but it was grace and not Gaius's existing merit that turned an ambitious, assassination-planning consciousness into one that honored the sanctity of another's life. It could have done the same for Marcus. The change of heart that saved Gaius from himself came from a level of awareness that went beyond his own conscious capacity to do good. Grace is like that. We must open the door to it, but it comes in and transforms us with a power that goes far beyond our own feeble and sporadic attempts at self-perfection.

As we have already seen, this transformation does not fly in the face of karma, but instead works in perfect harmony with it. That is why we can trace the law of cause and effect through the experiences of both Gaius and Marcus. As Figure 1 shows, both sets of experience fall completely within the lawful action of cause and effect. It must be that way; karma is a universal, undeniable law. Grace cannot turn it off. But grace can help us to make choices that activate the "positive return" aspects of karma rather than its corrective aspects, which we subjectively experience as "bad karma." This influence of grace cannot readily be observed from the outside looking in, for it has to do with inner changes of motivation. Yet, elusive as those subtle inner shifts of direction may be when we try to objectify them, we know them to be real enough when a sudden prompting from within turns us from the impulse to act unkindly or dishonestly or selfishly.

Freedom from "Karmic Debts"

Grace can free us from the necessity of "paying back" our "karmic debts." The Cayce readings suggest that while the law of karma makes for "meeting everything the hard way," through grace we "may take the choice that makes for life, love, joy, happiness" (no. 1771–2). Elsewhere these readings tell us that "karma may be lost in Him" if we will seek, follow divine guidance, and believe (no. 954–5). Many people consider this aspect of grace simply too good to be true. If the first version of grace appears on the surface to require too much good effort on our part for it to truly be grace, then this version appears to let us off the hook too easily, without enough trouble and toil. Yet if we look at the next shade of meaning for grace, "a state of reconciliation with God," we find a valuable clue as to how grace may indeed release us from our "karmic debts."

Reconciliation, the key word in the dictionary definition above, is itself defined in such terms as "to make consistent or compatible" and "to bring into harmony." If we look back to the purpose of karma, we see that karma also has harmony as its goal. If what we experience as "bad karma" is merely the goodness and harmony of this universe maintaining harmony with itself, then there is no longer any need for that "bad karma" once we are in a state of harmony or reconciliation. Through grace, we may experience that reconciliation through inner awakening rather than through the corrective effects of karma. As a graphic illustration of this aspect of grace, Figure 2 shows the intervention of grace after we have made a choice that, under karma, would have led toward corrective experiences—so-called "bad karma." Whenever we realize that we've done something out of harmony with God's law of love, and (to use a traditional theological term) genuinely repent of it, grace reinstates us so that there no longer exists the disharmony that would have summoned the karmic consequences in the first place.

This realization can occur relatively soon after the commission of the original act, or it may not happen until the soul has left the body and is evaluating its choices in the life just lived. If the soul is brought into a state of reconciliation before the karmic consequence has become fixed, there is the chance to transform that consequence into something more representative of the soul's new awareness.

Does that mean that grace lets us get away with whatever we want to do? That we can go our merry way, running roughshod over people, and still escape the consequences merely by repenting when it's all over? Implicit in such questions is the assumption that it is

Figure 2 Grace Intervening After a Negative Choice

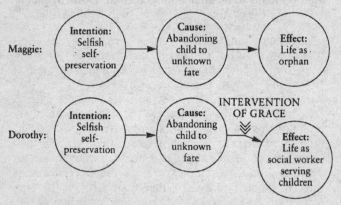

possible to hoodwink God and our own higher Selves. That by being crafty we can have it all. Such concerns usually arise out of an inadequate understanding of repentance and the soul-level awakening we are talking about here. Repentance is not merely hollow words of remorse, spoken the way many a child learns to say, "I'm sorry," to avert punishment. It is not crocodile tears shed in a moment of transitory compunction. Repentance reaches to the core of the soul, changing the way we think and the way we conduct ourselves. The literal meaning of the Greek word that is translated "repentance" in the Bible is "to turn around." True repentance, therefore, is not to cleverly dodge responsibility for our mistakes, but rather to claim responsibility so completely that no further action is needed to make us "own up" and do something about our transgressions.

It is on this principle that we can understand the contrast between the cases of Maggie and Dorothy, as given earlier in this chapter. Both souls made the same choice for the same reasons. Yet Maggie meets the consequences of this choice by experiencing in her next life what it means to be an abandoned child. Dorothy meets her karma by serving orphaned or abandoned children. The difference is not due to inequity in the law, but rather to the different responses of the two souls in question. The nature of Dorothy's follow-up life suggests that she had a soul-level awakening. That awakening led her to circumstances in which she could serve others in such a way as to demonstrate that she had learned her lesson.

Once again, karma has not been denied or suspended by grace. Both souls *are* meeting their karma. Both souls are paying for what they have done, but both are not "paying" in the way that such payment is usually thought of in karmic terms. From a purely karmic orientation, we may think of payment in terms of facing *retribution*. Under grace, payment can be made—with far more constructive results all around—through making *restitution*. And so, through grace, Dorothy pays her karma as a happy woman in a fulfilling career. Without grace, Maggie pays hers in sorrow and turmoil. If this seems unfair, we must remind ourselves that the choice in methods of payment was not imposed by God, but made by the souls themselves. The grace and the complete forgiveness it entails is always there; but it is up to us to accept it. Fortunately, it is never too late for us to make that choice, as we shall now see.

Experiences of Blessing

Grace can turn our experience of karmic results into experiences of blessing. We never reach a stage in our experience when it is too late for grace to transform it. Even as we are experiencing the results of karmic choices that have taken hold in our consciousness, heretofore unmitigated by grace, grace can still enter in and change the nature of our experience with that piece of karma.

For example, Cayce told one man that even though the physical condition he suffered was karmic in nature, he had a choice to make as to how he experienced that karma. He could consider it to be merely physical and seek physical means to alleviate his suffering, or he could realize that these conditions "can be met most in Him, who, taking away the law of cause and effect by fulfilling the law, establishes the law of grace" (no. 2828–4). He was further told to "lean upon the arm of Him who is the law" and through this experience "learn more of the law of the Lord."

Unfortunately, all of the questions this man asked in his subsequent readings concern physical treatments alone. He apparently did not respond at an inner level to this call to make his physical condition a lesson in soul growth. How many of us do, when faced with the burden, pain, or fear that serious illness entails? Yet there is no telling how such a shift in response to his karma might have changed this man's very experience of it. He may have found his condition healed, or he may have experienced a profound inner peace that transcended any distress his physical condition brought on. For under grace, the same karmic result that brings suffering and turmoil becomes an experience of meaningfulness and growth.

When we try to let grace into our lives to transform difficult circumstances we ourselves have created, it is sometimes hard to start with major conditions, such as serious illness. We can more easily release lesser emotional pain or turmoil to the healing influence of grace. Consider the case of a woman who, through personal past-life exploration, came to understand the karmic origins of her infertility. She knew that she had first built in thought—through past attitudes and behavior toward children—that which was now a physical condition. It was her karma. But, believing in the power of grace, she expected grace to eradicate that condition and give her and her husband the baby they so much wanted. She waited and waited, but still no baby came. She began to think that she would never truly open to grace in this situation, and that she would live out her karma in this life by experiencing the sense of lack and the emotional pain of remaining childless. Then suddenly, one day, all of her longing desire to have a child disappeared. She was free of it. Not that she reverted to the attitudes that brought her condition on in the first place, for now she understood what it was like to want a child and she knew she could respond to the appearance of one in her life with love and gratitude. But she also knew that her life had meaning just as it was, and she felt a sense of wholeness that previously would not have been possible without a child. Grace had entered her experience. Not in the way she had expected; not to reverse the physical condition her own past choices had created, but to completely transform her experience of them.

This aspect of grace may well be the one that is most easily grasped and experienced by the reincarnationist; as we have seen, the aura of meaningfulness that reincarnation casts around human suffering is often one of the very things that attracts us to the philosophy in the first place. But where a general sense of the meaningfulness in suffering comes with a belief in reincarnation, the transformation of a painful and personal experience into one of joy is the work of grace. This principle correlates with the last of the shades of meaning given in the dictionary's theological definition of grace: "spiritual instruction, improvement, and edification." When karma is turned into grace after the fact, it is always an experience in spiritual learning, coming to a deeper sense of what is important in life. When grace intervenes, the soul-level lessons that karma brings us seep into consciousness to some degree and allow a sense of meaningfulness to arise out of the very adversity we face.

Consider the scenarios relating to the experiences of Ned and Abel. Both are guilty of the same transgressions against humanity, and both meet the same karma. Unlike Dorothy, whose awakening happened in time to substantially alter the raw material of her subsequent life, Abel comes into his follow-up life facing the same karmic circumstances that Ned does. He suffers his karma, but something else happens as well. That suffering spurs him on to growth and transcendence. Even though his conscious mind might not carry the memory of his life as a slave overseer, the spiritual growth or edification taking place on a deeper level of consciousness is evidenced by the way Abel rises above his "fate" and becomes a force for good in his world. Abel may live a hard life, but he derives meaning from it consciously, even as the soul-level lessons are being learned. Ned's follow-up life illustrates the contrasting kind of experience, where there is no opening up to grace, conscious or otherwise. He lives out his karma, learning a valuable lesson on the soul level, but with no illuminating sense of meaningfulness or hope in his conscious mind. The contrast between the experiences of Ned and Abel are shown in Figure 3, which indicates the potential for grace to enter even after the effects of karma have come into manifestation.

We have now seen some of the many ways that grace can enter our lives and transform our experience. We have seen that the potential for grace is always there, that it is never too late to let the love and mercy of God alter the course of our lives. But we have also seen that our choice—our willingness to open up to, accept, or wake up to grace—is what draws the line between mere

Figure 3 Grace Intervening After Karmic Effect Was Manifested

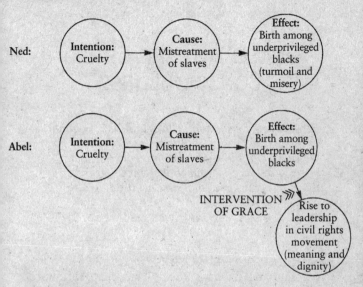

karma and karma that is redirected by grace. It is important, then, that we explore the nature of that choice, and develop a clearer sense of the awakening that it involves.

13

GRACE AND THE CHRIST CONSCIOUSNESS

For this is the evolution of the earth, the evolution of things, the evolution of ideas and of ideals. For, He came into the earth that through Him man might have access again to the grace and mercy of those spiritual forces that are the directing ideals of each soul-entity.

EDGAR CAYCE reading no. 3132–1

I HAVE USED THE WORDS "wake up" many times to describe what happens when we move into the awareness of grace. Yet I have also used the words "wake up" to describe what happens when a soul comes into the awareness that will bring on the corrective action of karma. In both cases, the awareness has to do with awakening to our innermost core of Oneness with the harmony and love behind this universe. But where the awakening that ushers in grace affirms forgiveness and fresh starts and wholeness, the awareness that brings on so-called "bad karma" recognizes the need for corrective action in our experience—action that we perceive to be painful or unpleasant. What is so different about these two forms of awakening? Why would they lead to such drastically different results?

Before we answer this difficult—but all-important—question, let's review the key concepts concerning karma and grace that we have considered thus far. We have seen now that both karma and grace are the expression of the goodness and harmony that is the ultimate force behind this universe. Both have to do with our Oneness with God, and both have to do with the love that the Creator has for his children. Furthermore, an inner awakening to that love and Oneness is necessary to our experience of both karma and grace. But where the awakening that brings karmic lessons into our lives involves the awareness that our negative choices have created discord with that harmony and Oneness, the awakening that brings grace affirms our unbroken unity with that harmony and Oneness.

In order to contrast the awakening that brings awareness of discord (karma) with the awakening that affirms unbroken unity with harmony (grace), we must go back to our earliest experience as souls, back to our original state and the choices we made as we began the process of individuation.

REEXAMINING OUR ONENESS WITH GOD

Our Oneness with God is a dominant theme in popular metaphysics. As we have already seen repeatedly, the Cayce readings are very much in accord with this concept. Our essential nature *is* one of unity with God and all of the love, harmony, and perfection that his nature carries within itself. On the deepest level, we do exist in unbroken unity with all that is good, whole, and eternal.

But we have also seen that our free will and our capacity to create have led to layers of separation *in consciousness* from our Oneness with God. These layers consist of our own creations in thought and materiality that we have come to confuse with our true identity. Thus, even though we have never stopped being one with God at the innermost level, we have stopped remembering it. Nor do we reclaim that memory simply

Figure 4   Layers of Self

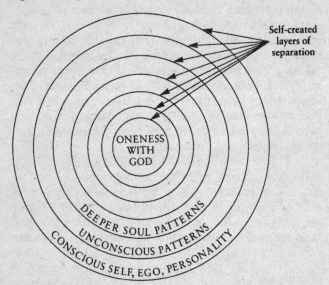

by accepting, as a matter of belief, that we are truly one with God. Even as I write these words affirming that Oneness, *I am not truly awake to my Oneness with God.* Therein lies the catch; therein lies the key to our understanding of the difference between karma and grace; and therein lies one of the great deceptions of popular metaphysical thinking. We are one with God, and yet we are not.

As long as we retain our self-created barriers of false identity, behavior patterns that are inconsistent with our Oneness with God, and habits of will that lead us away from rather than toward that Oneness, we are cut off from claiming our unity with God. In effect, we are not one with God—*in consciousness.* As Figure 4 illustrates, both our conscious and unconscious layers of self-created separation seal us off from our Oneness with God to the point that, from an experiential point of view, it might as well not be there.

What does all of this have to do with karma and grace? If we combine the notion of wakefulness (that is, "waking up" to grace or "waking up" to our disharmony") with the model we have just seen in the diagram above, we can develop an understanding of what happens on an inner level when we choose between mere karma and karma that is redirected by grace.

THE LEVELS OF SPIRITUAL WAKEFULNESS

Let's first look at what happens when we remain totally "asleep" to our true nature, our Oneness with God. We are completely out of contact with our Oneness with God at those times when our thoughts and actions are not in keeping with our true nature as children of God. As we set causes in motion that create disharmony with that Oneness, it is as though we thicken the walls of separation between our consciousness and our deeper awareness of Oneness. We become encrusted in our patterns of false identity to the extent that we perpetuate our discordant thoughts and actions.

Now it is important to keep in mind that it is totally possible (and even very common) for us simultaneously to think and behave in ways that are in keeping with our Oneness in some aspects of our life, while perpetuating disharmony in others. For example, one person might be the epitome of love and patience when counseling wayward teens or teaching the illiterate to read, yet be harsh, demanding, and judgmental when restaurant service isn't what it should be. Nor do these variations in the quality of our choices and responses occur only between distinct life areas. Sometimes there is a marked difference between the ways we respond to essentially the same situation at different times. To use a very simple example, if someone cuts you off in traffic, there are probably times when you take it in stride and do not feel even the inclination to respond in anger or resentment; yet there may be other times when rage and the desire to get even are the immediate and overwhelming response that you feel. Throughout the broad range of daily life experiences, there are times when our inner responses and the behavior we exhibit are in keeping with the love and harmony that characterize our core identity of Oneness with God. There are also times when our thoughts and actions encrust us deeper in our separation.

I am not talking about an all-or-nothing state of consciousness, where on one side of an imaginary line we would be classified as out of touch with our Oneness with God, and on the other aware of it. The level of our awareness of Oneness varies moment by moment, thought by thought, action by action. So when I describe what it means to be totally asleep to our true nature, I am describing what it means to be involved, in any given moment, in specific thoughts and actions that create barriers of separation from God.

As we have seen each time we have considered the law of cause and effect as the universe's natural force toward harmony, our good, harmonious, and constructive thoughts, words, and deeds multiply, while our inharmonious and destructive ones create discord. That discord will arise from our inharmonious choices, as surely as the sun will rise each day; but our awareness of that discord is related to our capacity to awaken to Oneness. That is, the deeper we are asleep to our Oneness, the stronger that discord will have to be before it jolts us into the awareness that discord even exists. By analogy, if you are very deeply asleep, it will take a very loud and strident alarm to break through to the sleeping consciousness and bring wakefulness. If you are in a very

Figure 5 Soul Awareness: Asleep and Awake

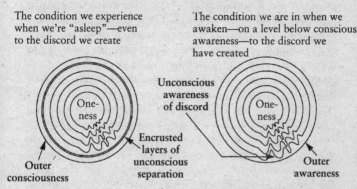

The condition we experience when we're "asleep"—even to the discord we create

The condition we are in when we awaken—on a level below conscious awareness—to the discord we have created

Unconscious awareness of discord

One-ness

One-ness

Encrusted layers of unconscious separation

Outer consciousness

Outer awareness

light sleep, on the other hand, you will awaken at the slightest sound out of the ordinary. In this same way, the more deeply encrusted we are in any undesirable pattern of thought or behavior, the more deeply we are asleep to Oneness—with respect to that particular pattern of separation. Sooner or later the discord will build to whatever level it takes to wake us up, and then we experience the corrective action of karma—the soul "takes on" its karmic lesson. Thus even the capacity to experience the law of consequences is a function of awakening.

Figure 5 shows the contrast between that state of consciousness we are in while we are perpetuating discord, and the state of consciousness we are in when we awaken to it enough to recognize—on the level of soul awareness—the discord we have created. Thus the experience of "bad karma" is a matter of awakening to Oneness just enough to know that we are out of harmony with it.

The awareness of grace is also an awakening to Oneness, but this awakening goes to a deeper level than that which brings on the corrective action of karma. It is an awakening that goes beyond the recognition of discord to "see" not only our core of Oneness, but also the fact that at the core our Oneness is unbroken and perfect. To put it another way, it is an awakening to the love, mercy, and forgiveness of God. Or, to put it yet another way, all separation from our Oneness with God is in consciousness only. That includes even the awareness of discord. Not that the discord we create is not real, or that it will go away if we just choose to disregard it; but, rather, at those moments when we awaken to the fullness of what Oneness with God really means, there *is* no more discord. Our consciousness has been transformed into one that experiences the Oneness, and at that point the discord is eradicated. We move into a state of grace. At that point, the so-called "karmic debt" does not have to be "paid," simply because it no longer exists as a condition of discord within our consciousness.

Once again, I am not talking about a one-time transformative experience that forever eliminates the need for us to "work out" our karma in life's difficult experiences. Nor am I talking about giving mere lip service to grace, forgiveness, and Oneness. It is simply not enough to say, "I choose grace" or "I have decided to let go of the consciousness that brings karma." The movement into a state of grace with respect to any of the multitudinous layers of separation that we have built (and continue to build) is a matter of a very deep-level soul awakening. It is a matter of claiming, moment by moment, a state of consciousness that truly apprehends Oneness and acts accordingly. It is a matter of experiencing that special state of awareness and expression that the Cayce readings call the Christ consciousness.

UNDERSTANDING THE CHRIST CONSCIOUSNESS

The Christ consciousness, as it is presented in the Cayce readings, has nothing to do with any particular religious persuasion, Christian or otherwise. It is a state of consciousness rather than a doctrinal position. In order to understand this distinction between religious belief and a state of consciousness, we might consider the relationship between belief in God and awareness of Oneness with him.

Awareness of Oneness, as we have already seen, is a matter of behaviors and attitudes. Many people who do not profess a belief in God may nonetheless frequently act with motivations that are very much in keeping with that core of Oneness. Others who do believe in God frequently act out of motivations that are not at all in keeping with the Oneness. In the same way, it is entirely possible for someone with no belief in the Christian religion to do a better job of expressing what Cayce called the Christ consciousness than some professing Christians might do. For some, a devout Judaism, Hinduism, Buddhism, or no formal religion at all might be the best path to Christ consciousness; for others, a Christian faith is the most meaningful approach.

Whatever form our beliefs might take, the Christ consciousness is about attitudes and behaviors that arise from an underlying consciousness that affirms Oneness and harmony. In order to better differentiate between this consciousness and other states of consciousness that we experience, let's look at a more specific definition from the Edgar Cayce readings.

Defining the Christ Consciousness

The most succinct statement that we have in the readings concerning the Christ consciousness was not made
directly by Cayce, but by his biographer, Thomas
Sugrue. Sugrue had been receiving a number of readings concerning the overall scheme of life, and from
these readings he tried to pull together a clear definition
of this state the readings were calling the "Christ consciousness." And so, using his best understanding of
what his readings had been saying, Sugrue constructed a
definition, which he then presented for comment during
a subsequent reading. Cayce's response to Sugrue's definition: "Correct! That's the idea exactly!" Let's look,
then, at how this definition of the Christ Consciousness
described it: "the awareness within each soul, imprinted
in pattern on the mind and waiting to be awakened by
the will, of the soul's Oneness with God" (no. 5749–14).

Virtually every aspect of this definition relates to the
major concepts we have been considering: our innate
Oneness with God, the mind's concern with patterns,
and the choosing role of the will. The only really new
element in this description of the Christ consciousness is
the reference to its being "imprinted in pattern on the
mind." What does it mean when we say that this awareness is imprinted on the mind?

In our earlier consideration of the mind's patterning
capacity, I likened the mind's patterns to roles in an
actor's repertoire. All of the many patterns of thinking,
behavior, and motivation that we have created over the
course of our history as souls exist within our deepest
soul-minds as "roles" that we choose (with the will) to
enact in response to the situations we meet in life. The
Christ consciousness is the role that exemplifies the perfect expression of our Oneness with God. It is an existing pattern of response, already created, and there for

us to tap into when we choose it. It is, in other words, imprinted on our deepest awareness.

How did it get there? That is the next mystery for us to unravel.

The Creation of the Christ Consciousness

Once again, we must go back to our earliest experience as souls if we want to trace the development of the Christ consciousness as a pattern imprinted on the mind of every soul. This time it is to the "rescue mission" that we turn our attention.

You will remember that once the first influx of souls had completely lost awareness of who they were, a second influx came in to the earth to remind them and lead the way toward spiritual maturity through true individuation rather than rebellion and separation. Although the second influx of souls came collectively as Adam in the five races of humankind, there was also an individual soul named Adam. This soul, as "captain" of the rescue mission, took on the task of working through the lessons of the soul in the earth. His experience took him through a series of incarnations until he had completed the cycle of earthly development. Like a trailblazer cutting the way through a thick and tangled jungle so that others can pass with relative ease, this soul worked his way through the entanglements of the earth, thus making the way clear for every soul. As many readers will have surmised by now, we know this soul best from his culminating incarnation as Jesus of Nazareth.

According to the readings, it was in his final incarnation as Jesus that the soul who began his earthly experience as Adam reached perfection, in the sense that he created the perfect pattern of what it means to be fully God and fully human at the same time. Another way to put it would be to say that he perfected the pattern of spirit expressing in matter. For the first time in Jesus, a soul experienced being in the earth without forgetting his true identity.

In the life of this soul who was in the process of completing a pattern that affirms Oneness with God over any false identities with a material consciousness, the cross represented the ultimate test of his willingness to crucify self for a higher good. In his acceptance of the crucifixion, he completed the work of atonement—at-one-ment between an individual soul in a flesh body and the deeper identity of unity with God. In essence, he rejected the false identity of material consciousness and in so doing brought to expression in the earth for the first time the truly individuated consciousness of a spiritually mature soul. He also overcame the limitations of materiality, as evidenced three days later by the resurrection of his body. Most important of all, he completed his work as captain of the rescue mission by creating this pattern of perfection for all souls to share in.

It is to this pattern we refer when we speak of the Christ consciousness. It is this pattern that is activated when we come into the awareness of grace. It is this pattern that redirects the paths of karma in the ways we have considered in the preceding chapter.

Just how does this work? How is it that a pattern of perfect Oneness that was brought to perfection by one soul has any influence on the rest of us? How did it get imprinted on our minds? Here, too, the answer lies in the concept of Oneness—this time not just our Oneness with God, but our Oneness with one another as well. Like points of a star that join in the common area at the middle, we are all connected with one another at the very deepest level, just as surely as we are connected with God. The pattern of perfect Oneness with God that was completed in the life, death, and resurrection of the soul we know as Jesus is now accessible to every one of us, by virtue of his connectedness with us. To use the language of the definition we began with, it is now "imprinted in pattern upon the mind." It needs only to be "awakened by the will" for us to move into the consciousness that ushers grace into our lives.

14

USING KARMA, CHOOSING GRACE

[He] through the varying activities overcame the
world through experience, bearing the cross in
each and every experience, reaching the final cross
with all power all knowledge, in having overcome
the world—and of Himself accepted the Cross.
Hence doing away with that often termed karma,
that must be met by all. The immutable law of
cause and effect is, as evidenced in the world
today, in the material, the mental and the spiritual
world; but He—in overcoming the world, the law—
became the Law. The law, then, becomes as the
schoolmaster, or the school of training—and we
who have named the Name, then, are no longer
under the law as law, but under mercy as in Him;
for in Him—and with the desires—may there be
made the coordination of all things.

EDGAR CAYCE reading no. 262–36

THE CHRIST CONSCIOUSNESS, as the ultimate expression of grace, shares in the paradox we have already considered: it is the unearned gift that we must nonetheless choose before it can become a reality in our lives. The pattern of Oneness with God is imprinted upon our deepest mind in spite of, rather than because of, what we have built with our minds and chosen with our wills. It lies there within our sleeping souls as a present from God, waiting to be unwrapped. We cannot create the Christ consciousness or orchestrate its influence on our experience, but we *can* remove the obstacles that stand in the way of its expression. In essence, we can choose the kind of thoughts and actions that open the way for this highest state of consciousness to flow into our awareness.

CHOOSING THE CHRIST CONSCIOUSNESS

The awakening of the Christ consciousness is a process rather than an event. It involves a gradual shifting of orientation, motivation, and behavior as we absorb the lessons of incarnation. We may experience instantaneous, isolated moments of awakening, but the *sustained* awareness of who we really are spiritually is the goal toward which all of our experience in the earth must eventually point us. We may cooperate with that process, thus hastening our spiritual awakening; or we may stubbornly dig ourselves deeper and deeper into the layers of separation from God. The choice is ours.

The Cayce reading excerpt at the head of this chapter can help us with this choice, for it carries a blueprint for the life that uses karma, chooses grace, and ultimately moves into perfect awareness of Oneness with God. If we follow it point by point, we can recognize key qualities of the life that is unfolding toward Christ consciousness. Let's examine this multifaceted reading in some detail, beginning with the first part of the blueprint, which has to do with overcoming the world.

What It Means to Overcome the World

In the first half of this excerpt, we see that the process of development that eventually led to the perfection of the Christ consciousness was one of overcoming the world. But notice also that this overcoming only came *through the various activities* in the world. Involvement within the material world, rather than a complete denial of it, is a necessary part of overcoming. The secret is not to eschew life in the earth, but to gain victory over blind identification with material consciousness.

This delicate balance between total rejection of the material world and becoming engulfed by it has been at the center of the soul's dilemma from the beginning. Souls were meant to go out and explore and become more complete by virtue of their experience—but they were not meant to lose their true identities in the process.

This delicate balance between rejection of the world and losing our spiritual identity to it also emerges as one of the common themes of human existence in both secular and spiritual literature. It is the story of Dorothy in Oz and it is the story of the Prodigal Son. E. M. Forster makes a potent statement concerning this delicate balance in his novel *Howard's End,* in which one of his characters, Margaret, ponders the question of how best to view the relationship between material and nonmaterial reality:

> The businessman who assumes that this life is everything, and the mystic who asserts that it is nothing, fail, on this side and on that, to hit the truth. "Yes, I see, dear; it's about halfway between," Aunt Juley had hazarded in earlier years. No; truth, being alive, was not halfway between anything. It was only to be found by continuous excursions into either realm, and though proportion is the final secret, to espouse it at the outset is to insure sterility.*

* E. M. Forster, *Howard's End* (New York: Random House, 1921), p. 195.

Continuous excursions into material and nonmaterial reality. A proportion (or balance) that cannot come ready-made but must instead be allowed to grow and unfold. These are the reasons that incarnation and all of the experiences it offers us are a necessary part of our individuation process. We did not come ready-made, but were instead given the freedom to *become* who we would be.

Pain and Struggle

Overcoming is sometimes a process of allowing pain and struggle to add depth to our being. We see, as we continue to follow the reading at hand, that the soul who perfected the Christ consciousness did so only through meeting cross after cross. The cross at Cavalry was not his first plunge into pain and despair in order to blaze that trail, but rather the final one in a series of tests and tribulations. Here, too, we can find some of the most moving statements concerning the meaningfulness of struggle and pain not in the volumes of theology or philosophy, but in the pages of the world's great literature. Consider this passage from George Eliot's *Adam Bede*. It begins at a stage late in the story, when the title character is beginning an upward climb following a great loss in his life:

> For Adam, though you see him quite master of himself, working hard and delighting in his work after his inborn inalienable nature, had not outlived his sorrow—had not let it slip from him as a temporary burthen, and leave him the same man again. Do any of us? God forbid. It would be a poor result of all our anguish and our wrestling, if we won nothing but our old selves at the end of it—if we could return to the same blind loves, the same self-confident blame, the same light thoughts of human suffering, the same frivolous gossip over blighted

human lives, the same feeble sense of that Unknown
towards which we have sent forth irrepressible cries in
our loneliness. Let us rather be thankful that our sorrow
lives in us as an indestructible force, only changing its
form, as forces do, and passing from pain into sympathy
—the one poor word which includes all our best insight
and our best love.*

Like Eliot's Adam, the Adam who represented all souls
coming into the earth reached the fullness of love
through the sorrows and trials he endured. As the writer
of the Epistle to the Hebrews put it, "For it became him
. . . in bringing many sons unto glory, to make the captain of their salvation perfect through sufferings"
(Hebrews 2:10). This too is part of the pattern, part of
what the Christ consciousness entails. If we can allow
the sorrow and pain that comes into our lives to make
us deeper, more compassionate beings, then we will
have learned one of the great secrets of life on earth.

The Paradox of Karma

Karma is immutable, and yet it can be "done away
with." Here we see what should by now be a familiar
paradox. We are told within a few short lines that the
law of cause and effect is immutable, and yet we are told
that it is done away with and that we no longer have to
be "under" it.

This echoes what we have already seen with respect
to the relationship between karma and grace: the awakening to Oneness that grace entails does not do away
with the lawful action of karma, but redirects it. It helps
us have a change of heart that leads to a different choice
than we originally would have made, thus setting a dif-

* George Eliot, *Adam Bede* (New York: The Modern Library,
1940), p. 353.

ferent quality of cause-and-effect action in motion. It brings a change in consciousness that reharmonizes us with our Oneness with God, thus averting the karmic result a destructive choice would have brought about. Or it alters the way we look at those conditions that have already manifested in our lives as the result of past destructive choices, thus changing our experience from one of pain or turmoil to one of deep meaning.

In short, in every case where grace operates in our lives, cause and effect also operates. It is just that the quality of cause-and-effect action is substantially different when grace is the motivating force. And, according to the reading above, what we must do in order to come under grace and mercy rather than "law, as law" is to "name the Name."

What It Means to "Name the Name"

Elsewhere in the readings we are told that the word "name" refers to our spiritual identity, the same way that our common names identify us from a material point of view. Each of our incarnations figuratively bears a name, or overall sense of identity—a label, if you will—that represents the quality of that life.

The "Name" is then another expression for the identity of perfect incarnation that is associated with the Christ consciousness. It is Oneness with God expressed within a fully individuated soul consciousness. When we "name the Name" we are essentially taking on and adding to our own consciousness the spirit and motivational quality that the Christ consciousness entails. By this approach, we could say that awakening to grace is a matter of allowing a new set of motivations to operate within us.

We took a passing look at this same idea back in chapter six, when we considered the questions of moti-

vation surrounding the law of positive return. At that
time we saw how, even though knowledge of return was
not the very highest of motivations, it was a good and
growth-promoting move toward the eventual adoption
of less self-oriented motivation. The reading above expresses this same idea in its reference to the law of
karma as a "schoolmaster."

Using the Law of Karma as a "Schoolmaster"

Under the workings of cause and effect, we learn under
the restraints of law to do the constructive things that
we must eventually do because of an inward motivation
that arises naturally from our very nature. Just as training wheels will hold a youngster's bicycle in balance until he gets the sense of inner balance that enables him to
peddle along effortlessly, the law of cause and effect
holds us in balance with the harmony of the universe
until we get the knack of it and harmony flows from our
very nature.

The difference between law-motivated behavior and
behavior that flows from our inner nature is like the
difference between not shoplifting because we are
afraid we will get caught, and not shoplifting because
there is no desire to steal. It is like the difference between visiting a friend in the hospital because you know
that it could just as well be you someday, hospitalized
and wanting company, and visiting because you want to
brighten your friend's day. It is like the difference between refraining from speaking unkindly of another person because you know that such behavior is wrong, and
never feeling the unkind inclinations in the first place.

I am not saying that the law-motivated behavior is
wrong or that it would be more honest to refrain from
those actions until the motivation was perfect. In every
case, the law-motivated behavior is good and ethical and

moral. Following the law is a training process that gets us in the habit of doing the right thing. But eventually we must grow into an even higher morality that needs no law to enforce it. We must come to the point of loving because it is our nature to love rather than because loving is the spiritual way to behave.

THE LAW WRITTEN ON THE HEART

This deepest of spiritual truths is the substance of that great prophecy of Jeremiah (31:33–34) which heralds the day when, "After those days, saith the Lord, I will put my law in their inward parts, and write it in their hearts; and will be their God, and they shall be my people. . . . for they all shall know me . . . for I will forgive their iniquity and remember their sin no more." The law written on the heart is the epitome of inward motivation, and it is another way of describing the Christ consciousness.

The attainment of that inward state of motivation that bespeaks our true identity is not a one-time achievement. It is a series of choices every day to live and think and *be motivated* by the memory of who we really are, rather than by false identification with the creations of material consciousness. As the Cayce reading that has been our blueprint for choosing the Christ consciousness expresses it, it is a combination of God's mercy and our *desires* that brings the "coordination of all things," that is, the claiming of our full Oneness.

Like the man who said to Jesus, "Lord I believe; help thou mine unbelief" (Mark 9:24), we do and at the same time we do not truly believe in our Oneness with God. The pattern is there in every one of us, imprinted on our minds, but we must learn to choose grace. Not as a matter of lip service, but choosing it with the quality of life that we live and in "naming the Name"—claiming our true spiritual identities.

It is not enough to choose with our conscious minds, our intellects, or even our emotions. We must choose it from the core of our being. Sometimes this means doing what is right, according to law, until we get to know what it feels like to do it because we want to. Sometimes it means stopping long enough to remember the love and mercy and forgiveness of God. Sometimes it means slowing down long enough to commune with our inner Oneness through quiet moments of meditation, prayer, or reflection. But we will always know that we are doing it when our lives exhibit the eternal qualities of kindness, gentleness, patience, love, wisdom, and peace. When we can bring those qualities into our fully individuated consciousness, the detour of rebellion will be over; and we will be fit companions for the God of this universe.

SELECTED BIBLIOGRAPHY

Cayce, Edgar. *The Edgar Cayce Readings*. Volume 10, *Jesus the Pattern*. Virginia Beach, Virginia: A.R.E. Press, 1980.

Cerminara, Gina. *Many Mansions*. New York: New American Library, 1978.

————. *The World Within*. Virginia Beach, Virginia: A.R.E. Press, 1985.

Cranston, Sylvia, and Carey Williams, eds. *A New Horizon in Science, Religion and Society*. New York: Julian Press, 1984.

Head, Joseph, and S. L. Cranston, eds. *Reincarnation in World Thought*. New York: Julian Press, 1967.

MacGregor, Geddes. *Reincarnation in Christianity*. Wheaton, Illinois: Quest Books, 1978.

Shelly, Violet. *Reincarnation Unnecessary*. Virginia Beach, Virginia: A.R.E. Press, 1979.

Sparrow, Lynn. *Edgar Cayce and the Born Again Christian*, Part Four, "Reincarnation and Christianity." Virginia Beach, Virginia: A.R.E. Press, 1985.

Stevenson, Ian. *Twenty Cases Suggestive of Reincarnation*. Charlottesville, Virginia: University of Virginia Press, 1974.

Sugrue, Thomas. *There Is a River*. Virginia Beach, Virginia: A.R.E. Press, 1973.

INDEX

ABOUT THE AUTHOR

Lynn Elwell Sparrow has been lecturing and writing on the subject of reincarnation for more than ten years. She chaired the task force that developed the popular Cayce home study course, "How to Discover Your Past Lives," and has conducted seminars on "Remembering Past Lives" in cities all across the United States and Canada. She makes numerous television and radio appearances each year.

Sparrow is also the author of *Edgar Cayce and the Born Again Christian,* which offers a correlation of Cayce's readings with the tenets of conservative Christianity. She is the author of the home study course, "Meditation Made Easy," and has written numerous articles on such topics as dreams, psychic experience, and holistic health.

First introduced to the Edgar Cayce readings in 1969, Sparrow spent ten years on the staff of the Association for Research and Enlightenment (A.R.E.). Her work with A.R.E. included public relations, speaker training, curriculum development and administration. She is currently a freelance writer and speaker and lives in Virginia Beach, Virginia, with her husband, Scott, a licensed professional counselor who uses holistic approaches to psychological and spiritual well-being.

THE HEALING WORK OF EDGAR CAYCE
CONTINUES

In the more than fifty years since Cayce's death, the organization he founded in 1931 has continued his efforts in helping people to understand the purpose of life and the universal laws that shape our experiences. You can get free information about the Association for Research and Enlightenment (A.R.E.) in Virginia Beach, Virginia by calling its headquarters: 1–800–333–4499.

The A.R.E. sponsors conferences and lectures throughout the U.S. and Canada on many aspects of reincarnation, karma, grace, and healing. A considerable portion of the Cayce readings deal with a holistic perspective of health and the healing process, including Cayce's unique view of the role of past-life influences upon our present day health. The A.R.E. Headquarters—where visitors are always welcome—includes one of the finest specialized libraries to be found anywhere in the world.

For those who choose to become members of the A.R.E.—joining a worldwide network of tens of thousands—additional resources are also available. The organization maintains a list of health-care professionals who are interested in applying the Cayce approach. Members can borrow detailed collections of what Cayce had to say about specific medical and non-medical subjects—more than four hundred different collections have been compiled and are available. You'll find fascinating subjects and life-changing ideas on a wide range of themes: dream interpretation, prophecy, reincarnation, meditation, spirituality, vocational guidance, ESP, intuition and dozens more. Members also receive a magazine, *Venture Inward*, which includes columnists and feature articles on how to transform one's own life using spiritual principles.

The A.R.E. offers study groups in most cities, many local regional activities, an international tours program, a retreat-type camp for children and adults, and A.R.E. contacts around the world. The Cayce materials also form an integral part of Atlantic University which offers a master's degree in Transpersonal Studies, with options to specialize in several areas.

For free information about any or all of these programs, call the toll-free number listed above or write: A.R.E. Department M, 67th and Atlantic Ave., Box 595, Virginia Beach, VA 23451–0595.